BRIAN J. L. BERRY

geography
of market centers
and retail distribution

Foundations of Economic Geography Series

PRENTICE-HALL

Foundations of Economic Geography Series
NORTON GINSBURG, *Editor*

Foundations of Economic Geography Series

Geography
of
Market Centers
and
Retail Distribution

BRIAN J. L. BERRY

Professor of Geography
The University of Chicago

PRENTICE-HALL, INC., Englewood Cliffs, N.J.

PRENTICE-HALL INTERNATIONAL, INC., *London*
PRENTICE-HALL OF AUSTRALIA, PTY. LTD., *Sydney*
PRENTICE-HALL OF CANADA, LTD., *Toronto*
PRENTICE-HALL OF INDIA PRIVATE LTD., *New Delhi*
PRENTICE-HALL OF JAPAN, INC., *Tokyo*

Foundations of Economic Geography Series

Among the various fields of geography, economic geography, perhaps more than any other, has experienced remarkable changes within the past twenty years—so many that it is almost impossible for one scholar to command all aspects of it. The result has been increasing specialization on the one hand and, on the other, a fundamental need for bringing the fruits of that specialization to students of economic geography.

The *Foundations of Economic Geography* Series consists of several volumes, each focusing on a major problem in economic geography. It is designed to bring the student, whether novice or more experienced, to the frontiers of knowledge in economic geography, and in so doing, forcefully to demonstrate the methodological implications of current research —but at a level comprehensible even to those just becoming aware of the fascinating problems in the field as it is developing today.

Each volume stands as a contribution to understanding in its own right, but the series as a whole is intended to provide a broad cross-section of on-going research in economic geography, stemming from concern with a variety of problems. On the other hand, the series should not be regarded as a complete synthesis of work in economic geography, although the volumes explore in depth certain major issues of keenest interest to economic geographers and others in related fields to a degree impossible in textbooks that attempt to cover the entire field. At the same time, the student is brought face-to-face with the kinds of intellectual and conceptual problems that characterize economic geography in a way that no over-all survey can accomplish. Each volume thus provides a basis for an intensive exploration of issues that constitute the cutting edge of research in this most dynamic and demanding field of knowledge.

As time goes on and new volumes appear in the series, the original volumes will be modified in keeping with new developments and orientations, not only in economic geography, but in the field of geography as a whole. The first volume to appear in the series, Wilbur Zelinsky's *A Prologue to Population Geography,* acts as a bridge between economic and cultural geography and as a means for exploring ideas and methods concerning a problem of increasing interest to geographers and social scientists alike: the growth, diffusion, and distribution of populations throughout the world. Brian J. L. Berry's *Geography of Market Centers and Retail Distribution* attempts to fill a major lacuna in the literature of economic geography, as it lays down principles concerning the spatial distribution and organization of marketing in both advanced and lesser developed economies. In so doing, it provides a bridge between the geographies of consumption, production, and cities, and links them for perhaps the first time effectively through a theoretical system, still primitive, but far in advance of comparable formulations.

Gunnar Alexandersson's *Geography of Manufacturing* reflects the need for considering the historical-ecological settings within which manufacturing enterprises originate and flourish. Though superficially nontheoretical, it contains flashing insights into the extreme socioeconomic complexities that have resulted in the world pattern of manufacturing, and it is concerned with an interpretation of that pattern through an evolutionary-descriptive technique applied to selected industries and regions.

Richard S. Thoman and Edgar C. Conkling in their volume on international trade deal with a topic that has not been given the attention it deserves by economic geographers. By careful analysis of trade data and an imaginative use of graphic and tabular devices, they interpret the pattern and structure of international trade in terms of current monetary and economic blocs. The result is the first modern treatment of one of the basic types of international relations, and thereby an important contribution to the political as well as economic geographical literature.

The other volumes in the series, whether concerned with transportation, energy, resource management, water, wholesaling, or agriculture, display "bridging" qualities that transcend the narrow limitations of ordinary descriptive handbooks. All are concerned with the new and the fresh as well as the traditional, and with the transformation of a somewhat parochial field of scholarship into one that is interdisciplinary as well as innovative and pioneering.

NORTON GINSBURG

The University of Chicago

Preface

The thesis of this book is that the geography of retail and service business displays regularities over space and through time, that central-place theory constitutes a deductive base from which to understand these regularities, and that the convergence of theoretical postulates and empirical regularities provides substance to marketing geography and to certain aspects of city and regional planning.

The order of presentation mirrors this thesis. Terms and regularities are introduced by examining several case studies in the United States in historical and cross-sectional detail. Central-place theory is next developed in both classical and modern forms. A study of origins (adding the depth of longer time spans) and of cross-cultural contrasts (adding the perspective of alternative value systems) follows; and, finally, the predictive procedures of applied marketing geography and the prescriptive aspirations of the planner are set within the frame.

This organization is not accidental. It stems from several years of experimenting with ways to present both classical and the very latest ideas to beginning students quickly, yet without sacrificing rigor, and it accords well with the aim of this Foundations series to combine both the established concepts and the latest ideas in a way that will bring the beginning student to the frontiers of geographic knowledge.

In reading the book, the student should proceed slowly and carefully, making sure that he understands the concepts and generalizations as they are presented, for later parts depend upon what has gone before. Some pains should be taken to study each of the maps and diagrams, because they are integral elements of the whole. Some parts of the volume use simple mathematics. If the diagrams are studied as directed, however, neither student nor teacher should have difficulty with the equations, for each is illustrated with an example. The only exceptions occur in Chapter 4, which considers important modern theoretical contributions. In the second half of this chapter the materials will probably be beyond the beginning student, but since they follow logically from the basic concepts, they will be available to him in a consistent frame as he proceeds to more advanced studies.

References to the theoretical and empirical literature will be found in the footnotes. A separate selected bibliography is not provided because it will be to the advantage of the student to study the complete source-book *Central Place Studies: A Bibliography of Theory and Applications* [1] in conjunction with this book.

I trust that I have given adequate thanks elsewhere to the many friends and colleagues who have helped me at various stages of the speculation, review, and empirical work on which this study is based. The support of the Geography Branch, United States Office of Naval Research under contract NONR 2121-18, NR 389-126, in the comparative empirical studies reported in Chapters 1 and 2 is gratefully acknowledged. Thanks are also due the Social Science Research Council under an Auxiliary Research Award that made possible the assembling of some of the historical materials and the exploration of the planning applications. Finally, the Social Science Research Committee of The University of Chicago supported the study of cross-cultural contrasts.

BRIAN J. L. BERRY

---

[1] By Brian J. L. Berry and Allan Pred (second printing with revisions through 1965). Philadelphia: Regional Science Research Institute (G.P.O. Box 8669), 1965.

Contents

Geography
of
Market Centers
and
Retail Distribution

PART 1 *definitions and examples*

CHAPTER ONE

Systems of central places in complex economies

Introduction

In complex, economically advanced societies we are accustomed to thinking of extreme division of labor, and to differentiating among the activities of production, distribution (exchange), and consumption. It is in the system of *exchange*, through the process of *distribution,* that the supplies of producers and the demands of consumers are brought together. In this sense, the interconnections of the exchange network are the strands that hold society together.

Exchange takes place in *markets*. Markets exist where a number of buyers and sellers communicate, and the price offered and paid by each is affected by the decisions of the others. A market, then, is a system which produces self-regulating prices; the prices, in turn, are the mechanisms connecting individual actions of choice.

In this general sense there are *world markets* for wheat or copper. Most types of exchange, however, involve a specific *market place.*

Market places are sites with social, economic, cultural and other referents where there are a number of buyers and sellers, and where price offered and paid by each is affected by the decisions of the others.[1]

The Chicago wheat pit and the London metals exchange are dramatic examples of market places of international significance, yet equally important are the hundreds of thousands of small *market centers* that dot the globe. Although they are seldom imposing, it is in these market centers that the daily process of exchange takes place. Whether they be

---

[1] Cyril S. Belshaw, *Traditional Exchange and Modern Markets* (Englewood Cliffs: Prentice-Hall, 1965), p. 8. See also Paul Claval, *Géographie Générale des Marchés* (Paris: Les Belles Lettres, 1962).

periodic markets in rural China or North Africa, villages and towns in the American Midwest, a dramatic new shopping center, or a decaying central business district, these market centers are the places to which consumers travel to complete the exchange process. It is in these centers, in effect, that demands and supplies must ultimately be brought into balance through the price mechanism. Producers and consumers come face to face in retail stores; retail and service businesses are the end of the chain of production and distribution, and the beginning of the process of consumption. It is in the *geography of retail and service business* that we find the vital, equilibrating interface between the *geography of production,* long a topic of professional interest and study, and the as-yet little developed *geography of consumption.*

The intermeshing of these geographies can be conceived in this way. Any economic system comprises a set of individuals who are the consumers of what is produced and, at the same time, the producers of what is demanded. In complex societies there is extreme division of labor. People specialize and regions specialize, yet individuals of similar income levels tend to demand similar arrays of goods and services (*baskets of goods* or *market baskets*). Whereas the geography of production involves extreme regional differentiation of activity, the geography of consumption involves demands for similar baskets of goods that repeat themselves in many regions. A problem of *articulation* results, and it is dealt with by the system of exchange and distribution. Local collection points assemble the specialties of producing regions. Local distribution points import the goods and services consumers need from many collection points in other locales. Collection and distribution points interlock in a complex web of exchange. Collection may involve several steps, but ultimately, in the United States, metropolitan centers provide the points of focus. Similarly, distribution takes several steps, including both wholesaling and retailing, but metropolitan centers ultimately have this role, too. They serve as collection points for regional specialties, and as places where regional specialties are produced and then exported. They are assembly points for the goods demanded by their surrounding consuming regions and are also major consumers themselves, drawing in needed products from other cities. Intercity exchanges are the connecting strands of a complex economy, and the cities are the points about which such an economy is organized. It is in the cities that the geographies of production and consumption interlock.[2]

Major metropolitan centers not only store specialties but also wholesale the products they have assembled to smaller surrounding urban places, which ship them to even smaller places, the market centers consumers visit to purchase the goods and services they need from retail and service businesses. The essence of the geography of retail and service business is the *clustering* of establishments in market centers visited by surrounding consumers. Retail and service business geography is thus inseparable from *urban and transportation geography,* because the commodity

[2] This discussion follows Otis Dudley Duncan, *Metropolis and Region* (Baltimore: Johns Hopkins Univ., 1960).

flows in a modern economy studied by the transportation geographer ultimately link producer and consumer, and are articulated by the network of cities and towns studied by the urban geographer. Cities and towns may arise as specialized producers themselves, but many are supported exclusively by their role as market centers. As such, they are neither more nor less than a cluster of retail and service establishments located in a place that provides a convenient *point of focus* for consumers who visit to purchase the goods and services they need.[3]

Centrality is the essence of the point of focus. Consumers who must visit the market place on a regular basis want a location that permits them to conduct their business with a minimum of effort, and if a choice of location is available will always prefer the one which involves least effort. Yet their business trips are varied. They are willing to travel only short distances to obtain items they need frequently. Less frequent purchases can often be postponed so that a single longer trip can accomplish several things—not only shopping, but socializing, entertainment, politics, and so on. For differing activities centrality therefore has meaning at different scales; in any area a *variety* of *central places* will thus exist. Businessmen located in some will attract consumers on a frequent basis, but only over short distances. Other places will be able to provide a greater variety of goods to much wider areas. The clusters of activity in these places vary, along with the sizes of the urban places in which the markets locate.

Central-place theory is the theory of the location, size, nature, and spacing of these clusters of activity, and is therefore the theoretical base of much of urban geography and of the geography of retail and service business. The next step is to describe the basic ideas of this theory by way of examples.

Background to Examples

Figure 1.1 identifies the areas of the United states which will be used for most of the initial exemplification. These areas provide a cross section of mid-continent America. Area 1 on the map spans the city and suburbs of the Chicago metropolitan area. Area 2 typifies the corn-growing, meat-fattening Midwest, lying between Omaha–Council Bluffs to the west and Des Moines to the east, in southwest Iowa. Areas 3 and 4 are in South Dakota. The former includes wheat-growing and cattle-raising counties centering on Aberdeen in the northeast, while the latter spans both rangelands north and east of Rapid City and the mining, forest, and recreation areas of the Black Hills to the west of that city, extending to the western borders of the state.

Each of these areas was analyzed in detail (using extensive field work) in 1960 in a study designed to evaluate the properties of central-place

---

[3] All other characteristics of centers derive from the cluster of activities: population depends upon the employment provided, and further local retail provision depends upon the population supported. Where large enough, the local population will generate a system of business centers serving consumers within the city.

Fig. 1.1. Case study areas.

systems in a variety of different locations, and to compare the properties in the various areas. An initial report was made on these studies in 1962.[4] Subsequently, both the city of Chicago and its metropolitan area were examined in much greater depth,[5] and the further insights of these later studies and a period of reflection are brought to the revised presentation that follows.

Most of the terms and concepts of central-place theory can be introduced by looking at the southwestern corner of Iowa shown in Figure 1.2. Several reasons exist for examining this area in some detail. First, Iowa has been the traditional, classic area for study of central places in the United States, because scholars thought that it satisfied the assumptions of central-place theory more nearly than any other region in North America. Second, to complete the picture are available not only the original field investigations of 1960 and the subsequent analysis, but also studies of the development of market centers in the area,[6] and a unique record of farmers' shopping preferences in 1934 in a form making possible direct comparisons with the 1960 studies.[7]

The essence of this information about the area is that, at any point in time, the geographic distribution of retail and service business in central places approximates an equilibrium adjustment to the geographic distribution of consumers. However, through time there have been continual

[4] Brian J. L. Berry, *Comparative Studies of Central Place Systems,* final report of Project NR 389-126, NONR 2121-18 (Washington, D.C.: U.S. Office of Naval Research, Geography Branch, February, 1962).

[5] Brian J. L. Berry, *Commercial Structure and Commercial Blight,* Department of Geography Research Paper No. 85 (Chicago: Univ. of Chicago, 1963); Berry, *Metropolitan Planning Guidelines: Commercial Structure* (Chicago: Northeastern Illinois Planning Commission, 1965).

[6] John A. Laska, Jr., *The Development of the Pattern of Retail Trade Centers in a Selected Area of Southwestern Iowa.* Unpublished master's thesis, University of Chicago, 1958. Laska used Dun and Bradstreet reference books to identify places with retail stores. Because of the limitations of the data, he had to restrict himself to places with grocery and clothing stores.

[7] The Bureau of Business and Economic Research of the University of Iowa has on file a complete set of manuscript "Community Service Survey Maps" for the state. These were completed by W.P.A. workers in 1933–1934, and record where farmers shopped for a variety of different goods and services, plus their trade center preferences. These data were available for the southwest Iowa area, and could be mapped in a manner exactly comparable to the consumer preference maps of 1960.

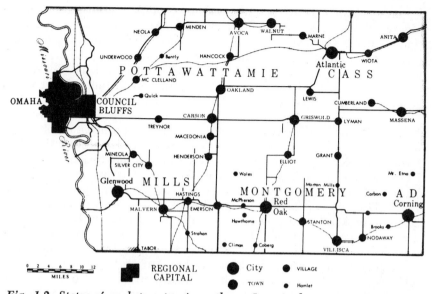

Fig. 1.2. *Status of market centers in southwest Iowa in the summer of 1961.*

adjustments in the pattern of business and centers in response to changes in the distribution and characteristics of consumers and in the technology of retailing. Progressive settlement was accompanied by spread of centers, and increases in population by increasing numbers of places, to a zenith around 1900. Subsequently there has been a thinning of the system of centers, because of changes in agriculture, loss of farm population, changes in consumer mobility making it possible to travel further, and increasing scale of retailing.

Central places for the farming population were provided by points of focus that initially were *not* associated with retailing. Grist mills, post offices, county seats, and railroad stations created a variety of meeting places for farmers; enterprising businessmen could take advantage of the superior accessibility to the consuming population that such locations provided. Combinations of the elements led to greater centrality for some of the places, and provided excellent location opportunities for businessmen serving less frequent demands. Competition between emerging retail centers, in the framework of these differential opportunities, created the central-place system.

History of an Example

Since we are fortunate enough to have data for a long period of southwest Iowa's history, it will be possible to tell the story slowly, gradually becoming more specific about the area and more precise about the ideas and terms to be used later in the book. Such a study will be rewarding, for the story must have repeated itself many times as the frontier expanded westward. Thus, Figures 1.3 to 1.8 contain only those features essential to the narrative. They cover the entire area seen in Figure 1.2 east of the bluffs overlooking the Missouri River, so that all centers except Glenwood and Omaha–Council Bluffs ultimately appear.

Although traders, agents, and missionaries had been in the area prior to 1846, the first white settlers did not arrive until the land was ceded to the United States by the Pottawattamie Indians in June of that year. The first settlers were Mormons, who established the trail west from Des Moines to what is now Council Bluffs, and created Omaha as their 1846–1847 winter quarters. When Brigham Young pushed further west, many of the Mormons remained in the area and established the first farms. In 1852 about half answered his call and left to join Young in Utah, but the other half remained in the area, forming the Reformed Mormon Church. Other white settlers also arrived in the period 1846 to 1851. These pioneer families provided most of their own needs, and the first land broken for farms was close to the woodlands which banded the area from north to south. However, they were not completely self-sufficient, and in the early years many of them traveled 100 miles south to St. Joseph, Missouri, or back east to Des Moines, to obtain corn and other necessities. Stores were built in Council Bluffs in 1847 to 1849 to cater to the increasing flows of westward migrants, and after 1849 there was rapid growth in Council Bluffs and Omaha as gold seekers streamed towards California. The first trade center serving the pioneer farmers was constructed in 1851—a general store selling dry goods and groceries. By 1868, on the eve of the opening of the railroads, a rudimentary set of centers had developed (Fig. 1.3). The woodland locations mirror the settlement patterns of the pioneers, and provide a good example of the first principle of central-place location: *consumer-orientation* of retail facilities. Market centers, and the retail and service businesses located in them, conform in their spatial pattern to that of consumers, because only those centrally located to markets can attract trade from consumers eager to economize on travel.

Often, in the early years, several stores would be established within

Fig. 1.3 (left). Rudimentary pattern of centers of 1868. Fig. 1.4 (right). Market centers in 1879.

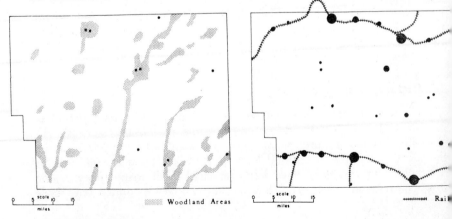

scale miles   Woodland Areas   scale miles   Rai

mile or so of one another, each providing approximately the same
oods and services. Competition would be intense, and success was often
ased upon the acquisition of some additional attribute of centrality. All
enters that survived were the sites of grist mills, which were basic
oints of focus for the pioneer economy. Perhaps the most important
dditional factor determining survival of a center was designation as
ıe county seat; political centrality provided added reasons for farmers
ɔ visit one center rather than another. Iranistan, Indiantown, and Lewis
ʾere founded in 1853–1854 within a mile of each other, but the first two
ʾere abandoned when Lewis was designated as Cass County seat.
imilarly, Frankfort flourished from 1855 to 1865, but was deserted after
ıe seat of Montgomery County was transferred in 1865.

The pioneer rural economy of the first quarter-century of settlement
ʾas transformed by the completion of railroads to Council Bluffs in
368 and 1869. Railroads provided the area with access to the market
:onomy of the nation, and the railroad stations were the collection and
ıstribution centers through which the connections were maintained.
armers began to specialize, using the railroad to ship their products
ɔ eastern markets. Other entrepreneurs were sensitive to the changes
. farmers' behavior. Towns, built in anticipation of the railroad, com-
ɔted for railroad stations because of the centrality to farmers the sta-
ɔns would provide. It was the railroad officials who most clearly saw
ɔe advantages to a town of having a railroad station; many of these
ficials were active in town promotion, and since it was they who de-
ʈrmined the precise location of stations, they profited thereafter. Atlantic
ıd Red Oak were both built in this way. Places in the vicinity of stations
ɛre abandoned as businessmen transferred their activities to the new
ıtion towns. Thus, Grove City vanished after the railroad's benefits
:crued to Atlantic. Size differences emerged among the station towns
ɔ some were designated county seats, and as some added processing
tivities to their collection and distribution functions. By 1879 the trade-
 nter system was almost completely railroad-oriented (Fig. 1.4).[8] This
ɔes not violate the previous argument about consumer-orientation, be-
use the most densely settled areas now followed the railroads, and
ps in the trade center pattern corresponded to gaps in the settlement
ttern, coincident, it should be noted, with inaccessibility to the rail-
ɪds.

After 1879 the settlement pattern filled in as more settlers came to the
ɛa, branch railroad lines were constructed linking the larger main line
ʋns, and a system of rural roads linked farms to markets and markets
ɔ each other. The number of market centers increased in direct response
ɔ the population expansion and increase, and previously inaccessible
ɛrstices between the railroads were filled.

The patterns of 1904 and 1914 are seen in Figures 1.5 and 1.6, re-
ɔctively. Many of the centers created after 1879 were associated with
ʋ railroad stations. Griswold, for example, was built at the Atlantic–

---

[8] In Figure 1.4, as in Figures 1.5–1.7, the different dot sizes identify towns with
ʾ–4, 5–9, and more than 10 grocery and clothing stores.

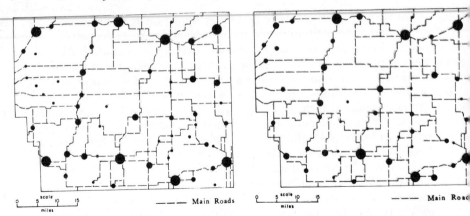

Fig. 1.5 (left). Relative importance of centers in 1904. Fig. 1.6 (right). Th
market-center pattern of 1914.

Red Oak midpoint, and Elliot at the station halfway between Griswol
and Red Oak. Wilson vanished when its post office was transferred t
Elliot. Lewis was fortunate enough to acquire the Atlantic–Griswol
midpoint. Railroad centers with branch lines radiating from them gre
more rapidly than those without them, and growth was even mor
rapid if the center was, additionally, a county seat.

Yet the period 1904 to 1914 saw the onset of new trends. Althoug
some new centers were to be established after 1900, the number of center
had actually reached its peak. The story changed from one of differer
factors shaping expansion, growth, and new center location to one o
competition and differential growth and decline within the existing s
of centers. All the existing centers possessed some modicum of centrali
in the local economy, as provided by the railroads, or in the politic
system, as provided by county arrangements. The grist mill declined
importance, and the introduction of rural free delivery after 1900 elim
nated many small post offices and made continuation of the stores ass
ciated with them unprofitable. Comparison of Figures 1.5 and 1.6 w
reveal a thinning of the market center pattern through elimination of th
smaller centers.

Tendencies toward differential growth and the thinning of the cent
pattern latent before 1914 were released by the coming of the automob
and paving of roads. Roads paved to make farms more accessible
their local market centers enabled farmers, in their cars, to bypass t
smaller centers and patronize larger centers. Use of trucks made possi
centralization of railroad collecting and distributing operations in t
larger stations, eliminating the centrality provided by the station
smaller towns. A process of differential growth started in which t
smallest centers vanished, the intermediate-sized places suffered a relati
decline, and only the larger centers grew. In the period 1914 to 19
all the trade centers that were abandoned lay on inferior roads with
nine miles of a major center. The few new centers to be established we
located at previously unoccupied paved highway intersections. T

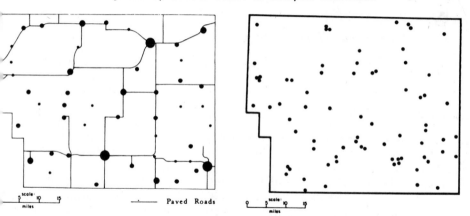

Fig. 1.7 (left). Relative importance of centers in 1956. Fig. 1.8 (right). Market-center failures, 1851–1956.

Paved Roads

centralization process was fostered by increased scale of retailing and he emergence of chain-store operations. Chains preferred larger centers, nd bigger stores had to locate in larger centers to survive. Figure 1.7 hows the resulting pattern in 1956. The largest centers are those which ombine all elements of local centrality: (1) political (they are county eats); (2) railroads (they are the main stations); and (3) market attractions, for they have been able, through their cumulative advantages, o provide the greatest variety of largest scale retail and service facilities, hus offering a more powerful appeal to consumers than their smaller ompetitors. The pattern to be seen is a product of multiple and changing lefinitions of access to consumers, and of the competitive advantages to erve these consumers accruing to those able to occupy or acquire the oints providing centrality to the consuming population.

Given the distribution of consumers, the pattern of market centers bserved today depends upon the successive (and for the major centers, umulative) definitions of points of access to the population: grist mills, ost offices, county seats, railroad stations, and paved highway inter-ections. Although a few individuals were able to use prior knowledge o locate successful enterprises before technology changed (for example, ie railroad officials), many who attempted to establish market centers iled in the competitive process because others had been lucky enough, r had the foresight, to select locations with greater centrality. There ere enough beginnings that failed for the pattern of market centers to ave developed into forms quite different from what we see today if ie factors giving definition to centrality had worked differently (Fig. .8). What is important is the competitive process that was working. hose who survived this process were those who best satisfied the rules : consumer-orientation by occupying locations of maximum accessibility. pportunities for development of activities in smaller places were de-rmined by their location relative to the larger and more desirable laces; this finely balanced interdependency is what has created the stem of central places we can observe in the area today.

Consumer Travel and Centrality

What do different and cumulative definitions of centrality mean in terms of the behavior of consumers? Some initial evidence can be provided for 1934, when a detailed survey was made of farmers' shopping habits. Responses to the question "Where do you obtain your . . . ?" for a great many goods and services, were recorded on manuscript maps; seven of these maps are presented as Figure 1.9(a)–(g). The mapping device used is the "desire-line," a straight line drawn between farm and market to indicate the farmers' shopping habits.

The first maps (a and b) exemplify the very local trade or service areas for goods, services, and facilities that can be provided at small scale and for which consumers were unwilling to travel far, either because of frequency of demand or bulk of the commodity. Later maps (c to g) show how centers with superior centrality extend their trade areas by capturing the trade of surrounding smaller centers for goods and services which must be provided at greater scale if they are to be profitable, which consumers are willing to travel over longer distances to obtain, and for which the most rational locations are in the larger centers. Thus, in Figures 1.9(e) and (f) only the county seats, with their many cumulative advantages, have significant market areas, and in Figure 1.9(g) even they defer to the regional capitals of Omaha–Council Bluffs to the west and Des Moines to the east in the matter of daily newspapers.

Several facts are notable about the successions of market areas: (1) they seldom overlap, except in a limited, peripheral "zone of indifference," so that consumers appear to be making systematic choices of the closest centers offering the goods they need (although in Figure 1.9(c), for example, the larger places with greater cumulative accessibility draw in

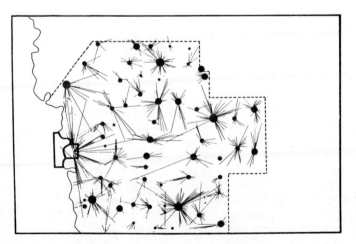

Fig. 1.9. Farmers' preferences in 1934.

(a) Church visited.

Fig. 1.9 (cont.).

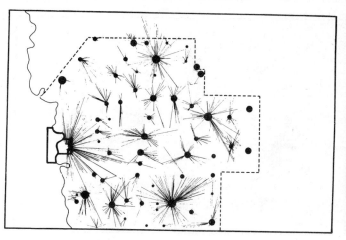

(b) Grocery shopping.

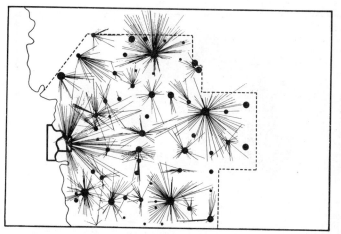

(c) Physician's office location.

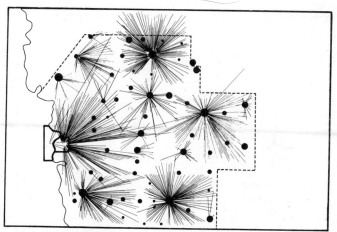

(d) Lawyer's office location.

Fig. 1.9 (cont.).

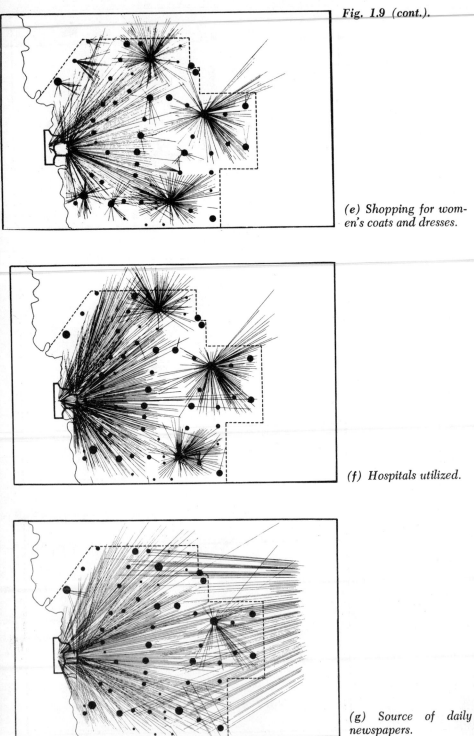

(e) Shopping for women's coats and dresses.

(f) Hospitals utilized.

(g) Source of daily newspapers.

consumers from longer distances); (2) "centers" are indeed close to the geometric center of their markets; (3) as scale requirements drop, businessmen are able to exploit the consumer desire to travel less to obtain what they need by "squeezing" small centers midway between larger places; and (4) small centers perform only a few limited scale activities, whereas large centers perform a range of activities and serve a variety of areas of different sizes. If a *system* is defined as an entity comprising interacting interdependent elements, then we certainly seem to be dealing with a *central-place system* of markets, consumers, and the multiple interactions and interdependencies among them.

The Central-Place System in 1960

The features of this system must now be spelled out more rigorously, making use of many kinds of interlocking data collected in 1960, including information on the retail and service activities performed by the centers, their market areas, and consumer shopping and travel behavior. Although surveys were made of the kinds of retail and service business provided by all the market centers shown in Figure 1.2, and sample studies were conducted of the market areas of business in each of these places, the limitations of time and effort dictated that intensive interviewing of farmers and town residents about their shopping habits and preferences be restricted to the "intensive" study area identified in Figure 1.10.

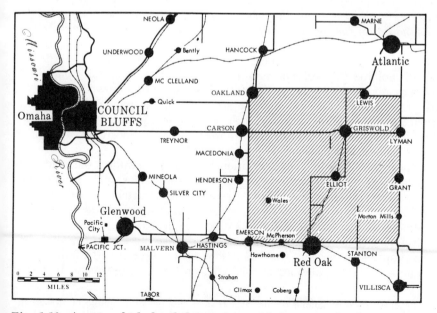

Fig. 1.10. Area in which detailed interviews with farmers and urban residents were made in 1960.

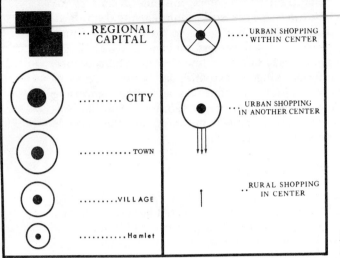

Fig. 1.11. Legend for Figures 1.12 to 1.19.

Residents of the area [9] were asked about the places from which they obtained many different kinds of goods and services. Four of these were selected: clothing, furniture, dry cleaning, and food. Separate maps are presented for shopping preferences of the urban and rural residents. Figure 1.11 is a legend of the cartographic conventions used. Desire lines again depict farmers' preferences as to center. Centers are scaled into five sizes (hamlets, villages, towns, cities, and the regional capital), corresponding to the levels or steps of the *central-place hierarchy*. Preferences of urban residents are shown by "wheels." If the commodity is purchased by one of the sample respondents in the town of residence, a spoke is added to the wheel. If another place is visited, an arrow is shown from one wheel to another.

The point of this series of maps is (1) to show the successive parceling of the area into a *hierarchy of central places;* (2) to show the *levels* of the hierarchy; (3) to examine the sizes of market areas and the nature of market area boundaries for each of these levels; and (4) to explore the locations of lower-level centers relative to the locations of higher-level centers and their market areas.

Given the ideas of consumer-orientation and centrality, the evidence concerning relative locations, levels, and hierarchies will include the assemblage of ideas needed to capture the character of central-place systems, which provide, in turn, the basic organizing scheme for understanding the geography of retail and service business.

Figure 1.10 shows several dot sizes corresponding to the *levels* of the central-place hierarchy. The *villages* of Elliot, Lewis, and Stanton, for example, have populations of 459, 501, and 514, respectively. In them

---

[9] A 10 per cent sample of the farmers, and a 5 per cent sample of the urban households.

are found 26, 24, and 21 different *kinds* of retail and service business, and 42, 43, and 28 different *establishments* (stores). Each has a maximum *market area* of approximately 70 square miles (consumers are drawn in from a maximum distance of about 5 miles), and in this area they reach another 500 to 600 people, so that total population served is 1,100 to 1,200. Synonyms often used for market area are the *service or trade area, hinterland* or *complementary region* of the center. Similarly, the maximum distance consumers are willing to travel to the center is often called the *economic reach* of the center, or the *range* of the largest-scale establishments located in it. Examples of the activities locating in each of the villages are: grocery, gas station, bar, restaurant, post office, farm elevator, and church.

Towns such as Griswold, Villisca, or Oakland form the next level of the hierarchy. They have populations of 1,207, 1,340, and 1,690, perform 50, 43, and 49 different kinds of business from 102, 90, and 97 establishments. Total taxable sales in 1960 were $2 to $2.5 million. Their maximum reach extends outward no more than 8 miles to a market area of 200 square miles containing an additional 2,500 to 3,000 consumers, for a total of 4,000 to 4,200 people served. In addition to the activities performed by villages, they provide such others as: hardware store, furniture and appliance store, complete drug store, doctor, dentist, dry cleaners, bank, insurance agent, and funeral parlor. These activities, since they cannot be provided profitably in the villages, which have too short an economic reach, are said to have greater *conditions of entry* or *threshold requirements* than the activities locating in the villages, or to be of *higher order* than those provided by the villages.

The third level is occupied by the *small cities*—county seats such as Atlantic and Red Oak, populations 6,890 and 6,421; 92 and 90 kinds of business; 411 and 312 establishments; maximum reaches of less than 20 miles; trade areas of 1,000 square miles containing more than 20,000 additional consumers, for total population served approaching 30,000. Sales in 1960 were $16 million in Atlantic and $14 million in Red Oak. In addition to the activities provided by the towns they offer such others as: county government offices, sales of jewelry, shoes, clothing of all kinds from both specialized stores and junior department stores, florists, liquor, ethical drugstores, movies, newspaper, sales of new and used autos and of auto accessories, and the like.

Two other levels are noted on the illustration: hamlets and the regional capital. The *hamlets* have up to 100 population, but seldom more than four or six and usually only one or two stores, such as a general store, farm elevator, gas station, roadside restaurant, or a bulk fuel depot. The *regional capital* of Council Bluffs–Omaha [10] reaches out for almost 40

---

[10] Actually, we should probably call Council Bluffs the *regional city* and Omaha the *regional metropolis*, for in other parts of the country these levels have distinct locations in the spatial system. The later discussion of the hierarchy as a spatial system differentiates the two levels. Depending upon the part of the country, either a regional city or a regional metropolis may be the acknowledged regional capital.

miles on the Iowa side of the Missouri River, to an area containing more than 100,000 people (within this area those to the north prefer Council Bluffs, but those to the south, who can reach Omaha without having to pass through Council Bluffs, prefer the larger city, although there are no differences in the eastward reach of the two). Sales in Council Bluffs alone approached $70 million in 1960, provided by over 1,100 retail and service establishments, including an array of department stores and specialty shops, professional services, and cultural facilities.

These are the levels of the hierarchy. Figures 1.12 to 1.19 reveal how they interlock in a *spatial system,* and Table 1.1 shows how they relate in an accumulative fashion.

Table 1.1.   Steps of the Hierarchy

Level of center

Order of function	Hamlet	Village	Town	Small city	Regional city	Regional metropolis	National metropolis
Lowest	✿	✿	✿	✿	✿	✿	✿
2		✿	✿	✿	✿	✿	✿
3			✿	✿	✿	✿	✿
4				✿	✿	✿	✿
5					✿	✿	✿
6						✿	✿
7							✿

* Indicates that a center provides this group of functions.

Figures 1.12 and 1.13 show how the two county seats and the regional capital attract customers from surrounding areas to purchase clothing. The residents of different urban centers show clear and almost perfectly mutually exclusive preferences, so that there is no difficulty at all in identifying the areas dominated by each of the large central places. Much the same can be said of the rural residents. Within the market areas that can be traced out on the map of urban preferences, the farmers make the same clear choice. There is only a little interdigitation along the boundaries, and right along the edge farmers said they visited both centers, indicating that market area boundaries trace out real lines of indifference in choice, the geographic equivalent of the economist's "indifference curves." Final points to note are that: (1) the regional capital draws consumers from somewhat further than the smaller county seats, and (2) towns, villages, and hamlets do not sell clothing because their maximum trade areas embrace too few consumers for clothing stores to be profitable ventures. In Figure 1.13 one or two trips to smaller centers to purchase clothing are recorded. These all involve older people who buy only work clothes sold by variety or general stores.

What happens to consumer preferences when the economic reach of the smaller towns is sufficient to support a store? Figures 1.14 and 1.15 provide the answer. Figures 1.14 and 1.12 are identical, except that Griswold consumers shop in their own town for furniture. In Figure 1.15, Gris-

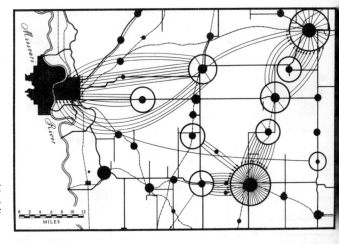

Fig. 1.12. Shopping preferences of urban residents: purchase of clothing in 1960.

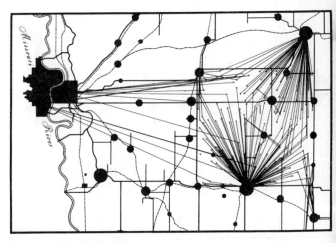

Fig. 1.13. Rural preferences: clothing.

wold is seen to attract farmers at the expense of both Atlantic and Red Oak, and to the southeast Villisca does the same at the expense of Red Oak in the interview area, and Corning (off the map). Drawing power for furniture sales is again related to size: (1) that of Omaha and Council Bluffs is greatest, and the variety and scale of offerings there are powerful enough to override such towns as Oakland, which draw in some consumers although they are unable to secure the more exclusive trade area of Griswold or Villisca; (2) the county seats of Atlantic and Red Oak have smaller market areas for furniture than for clothing because towns such as Griswold, located on the watershed between the market areas for clothing, are able to attract enough of the local farmers in that watershed zone to make the selling of furniture profitable; and (3) the towns of Griswold and Villisca now appear as centers, but with the lowest drawing power.

Dry cleaning is also an activity that can be supported by the intermediate-sized towns. Thus, Figure 1.16 is a repetition of Figure 1.14, except

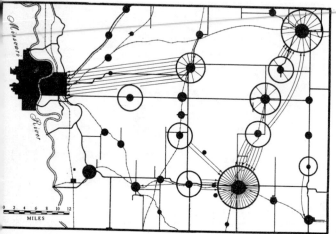

Fig. 1.14. *Urban preferences: purchase of furniture.*

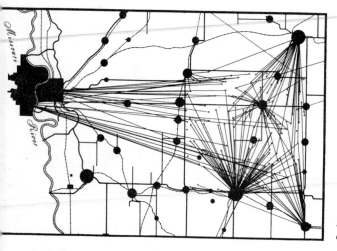

Fig. 1.15. *Rural preferences: furniture.*

for one or two long-distance arrows related to a weekly dry-cleaning pick-up service operating out of Glenwood. In fact, if *any* of the activities listed in connection with the towns had been selected, the maps would have been identical, because the *levels* of the central-place hierarchy are the result of the common behavior of consumers with respect to goods and services of the same *order*. Similarly, the types of business listed along with the description of the county seats would have produced maps identical to Figures 1.12 and 1.13.

One difference is to be noted between Figures 1.15 and 1.17, however. Trade areas of Atlantic, Red Oak, and Griswold are unchanged, but the reach of the regional capital into the western part of the interview area has been replaced by exclusive trade areas of towns such as Oakland. The difference stems from the nature of the two goods, furniture and dry cleaning. The former is demanded infrequently, and people like to shop and compare in stores which offer great variety; furniture is a *shopping good*. Dry cleaning, on the other hand, is a *convenience service*,

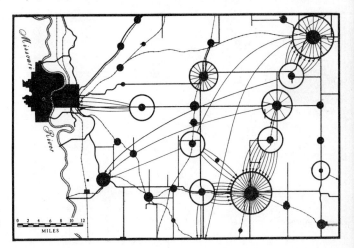

Fig. 1.16. Urban preferences: use of dry cleaners.

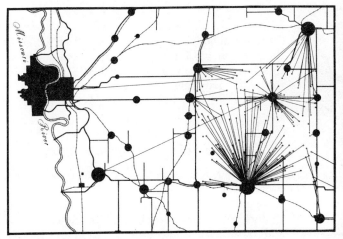

Fig. 1.17. Rural preferences: dry cleaners.

needed frequently, and not demanding comparison buying. The regional capital is able to extend its reach to 40 miles for shopping goods, but for convenience goods the advantages of proximity afforded by such towns as Oakland and Carson are critical, and these towns are able to attract enough consumers to make dry cleaning a profitable venture.

Figures 1.18 and 1.19 present a low-order village-level good, foodstuffs. Villages such as Lewis, Elliot, Emerson, and Stanton, located on the watersheds of the market areas described earlier for higher order goods (Stanton between Villisca and Red Oak, Elliot between Red Oak and Griswold, Lewis between Griswold and Atlantic, and Emerson between Red Oak and Malvern–Council Bluffs, as well as Wiota between Atlantic and Anita) are able to reach out for consumers and attract enough of them, by offering the advantages of proximity, to make grocery stores profitable. Note, therefore, that urban residents prefer to shop for groceries in the place in which they live (Fig. 1.18). Figure 1.19 shows the reach into rural areas to be a function of size. Villages attract fewer

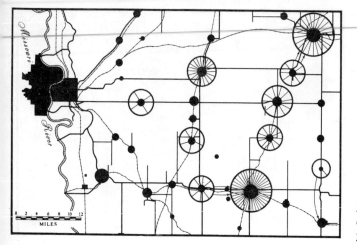

Fig. 1.18. *Urban preferences: purchase of foodstuffs.*

farmers over shorter distances than do towns, and towns in turn have shorter reaches than county seats, all of which corresponds neatly to the historical view of the cumulative advantages of the different places as foci for rural life. Careful examination of Figure 1.19 will also show the towns to have about the same trade areas as in Figures 1.15 and 1.17, so the villages have established market areas largely at the expense of the county seats.

The Hierarchy Is a Spatial System

These levels of centers define a central-place hierarchy in which there are distinct steps of centers providing distinct groups of goods and services to distinct market areas. The interdependent spatial patterns of centers of different levels, and the interlocking market areas of goods and services of related orders, weld the hierarchy into a central-place system.

Towns are located midway between the county seats, and villages midway between towns and county seats. As one travels along the highways between county seats, very regular progressions of places are encountered: county seat, village, town, village, county seat, all approximately evenly spaced (actually, the villages are likely to be a little closer to the towns than they are to the county seats).

At the order of goods and services appearing first in villages (i.e., those activities which can be performed profitably serving the consumers within the maximum reach of villages), centers of all levels have trade areas embracing the closest consumers, but those of villages are smaller than those of towns and county seats (5, 8, and 10 to 15 miles, respectively). The villages vanish from view when the next order of activities is examined, however, because they attract too few people to satisfy the threshold requirements of furniture stores or dry cleaners. The people who shop for groceries in the villages turn to the nearest county seats, so

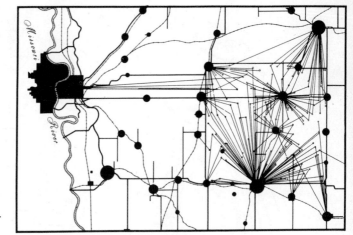

Fig. 1.19. Rural prefer-
ences: foodstuffs.

that market areas of towns reaching out 8 miles and those of the county
seats reaching out 15 miles are seen, with the regional metropolis reaching
out 30 miles for convenience and 40 miles for shopping goods of the town
level. Finally, insofar as the data are concerned, the towns vanish in the
sales of such commodities as clothing, shoes, and jewelry; their economic
reach is too small to satisfy the conditions of entry into retail business of
that kind. The county seats and regional metropolis reach out to embrace
the market areas of the towns, to distances of 20 and 40 miles, respectively.

Are the market areas of the county seats ever captured by regional
cities in the provision of yet higher order goods or services? Figure
1.9(g) shows how, even in 1934, Omaha–Council Bluffs to the west and
Des Moines to the east reached across the study area to sell their daily
newspapers. At that time Atlantic remained the only county seat to
publish daily, although other county seats did publish bi-weeklies or
weeklies.

The levels thus proceed upwards, and for the United States a complete
set includes hamlet, village, town, small city (county seat), regional city,
regional metropolis, and national metropolis. Sizes of the urban places
at each level vary from one part of the country to another, and are disturbed by the presence of manufacturing and other nondistributive
activities (disturbances, as we shall see later, are *relatively* greater for
the smaller centers). However, from the Iowan base, the size sequence
would be approximately 100, 500, 1,500, 6,000, 60,000, 250,000, and over
1 million persons; in terms of the orders of activities performed, the names
proposed by some authors for the levels of the village through the regional
metropolis are: local convenience center, full convenience center, shopping goods center, specialty goods center and secondary wholesale center,
and primary wholesale center.[11]

[11] John R. Borchert and Russell B. Adams, *Trade Centers and Tributary Areas
of the Upper Midwest* (Minneapolis: Univ. of Minnesota, 1963). They divide the

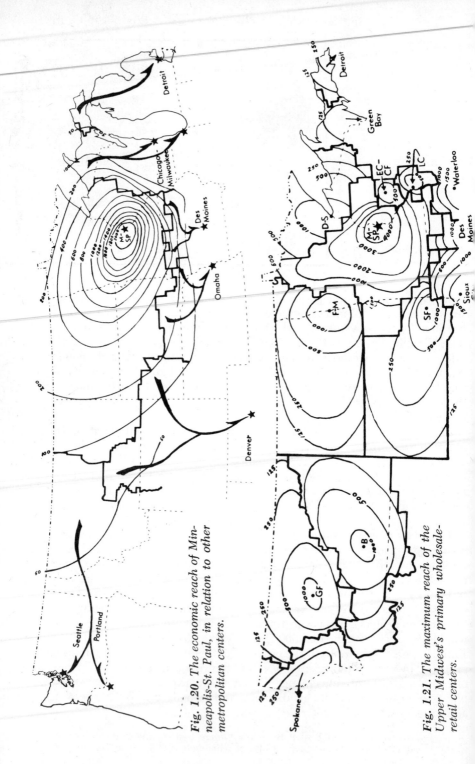

Fig. 1.20. The economic reach of Minneapolis-St. Paul, in relation to other metropolitan centers.

Fig. 1.21. The maximum reach of the Upper Midwest's primary wholesale-retail centers.

Figures 1.20 and 1.21 show the reach of primary wholesale centers and of the Twin Cities metropolis in the Upper Midwest. In this illustration, translated from the work of Borchert, communications data (per capita telephone calls from smaller centers to the primary retail-wholesale centers, and from the latter to the metropolis) were mapped to isolate market area boundaries; these boundaries were then adjusted to correspond with those of the counties.

Another way of viewing the interlocking systems character of consumer shopping behavior is shown in Tables 1.2 to 1.5 (pp. 24–25). These tabulations show the different orientations of farmers and urban residents within the maximum economic reaches of county seat Atlantic and town Anita. Variations among the tables are clearly a function of the levels of the hierarchy, with the reach of the metropolis being felt for the highest order goods. Atlantic is the dominant point of focus for the farmers in Table 1.2, although centers at lower levels compete within its maximum reach for lower order goods. The only leakages in Table 1.3 are from the pull of the metropolis in style goods. Farmers resident in the Anita trade area depend upon Atlantic for higher order goods, and Anita is dominant only at the next level down (Table 1.4). Again, the pull of the metropolis is felt for style goods. One caution should be noted in comparing these percentages with some of the previous data in this chapter. The trade area maps were based upon responses as to where consumers purchased *most* of a given commodity. The percentages in Tables 1.2 to 1.5 are based upon surveys by the Bureau of Business and Economic Research at the University of Iowa, which asked where the *last* transaction was made.

---

centers providing shopping goods into two levels, "partial" and "full." The latter correspond to Atlantic and Red Oak, county seats with a full range of shopping facilities, whereas the former might correspond to the next tier of county seats such as Corning (population 2,100, 70 central functions), Audubon (population 2,950, 66 central functions), or Guthrie Center (population 2,100, 65 functions), with greater ranges of activity than the towns but scarcely comparable to Atlantic. These smaller county seats are the ones which have been least successful in competing for the shopping goods trade of midpoint towns.

Table 1.2. Centers Used by Farmers Residing in Maximum Atlantic Trade Area

Percentage of farmers making last purchase in:

	Atlantic	Omaha-Council Bluffs	Smaller places ° or from catalog
Men's work clothes	92	1	7
Women's shoes	88	8	4
Men's shoes	86	4	10
Teenage girls' clothes	81	15	4
Children's clothes	79	7	14
Men's suit	72	16	12
Women's coat	68	23	9
Drugs	79	0	21
Groceries	66	0	34
Furniture	64	16	20
Farm machinery	62	1	37
Lawyer	87	0	13
Dry cleaning	80	1	19
Banking	70	1	29
Doctor	63	4	33
Hospital	63	25	12

° In Atlantic trade area.

Table 1.3. Places in Which Atlantic Residents Shop

Percentage of Atlantic residents making last purchase in:

	Atlantic	Omaha-Council Bluffs	Smaller places or from catalog
Men's work clothes	98	1	1
Children's clothes	94	3	3
Men's shoes	88	10	2
Women's shoes	88	11	1
Men's suit	81	17	2
Women's coat	73	21	6
Drugs	100	0	0
Groceries	100	0	0
Furniture	84	10	6
Banking	98	1	1
Dry cleaning	98	1	1
Doctor	96	3	1
Lawyer	96	1	3
Hospital	75	19	6

Table 1.4   Centers Used by Farmers Residing in Maximum Anita Trade Area

	Anita	Omaha-Council Bluffs	Atlantic	Other
	Percentage of farmers making last purchase in:			
Men's work clothes	47	0	51	2
Men's suit	31	16	49	4
Children's clothes	30	7	48	15
Men's shoes	28	7	63	2
Teenage girls' clothes	17	0	83	0
Women's shoes	15	4	76	5
Women's coat	2	22	74	2
Drugs	87	0	13	0
Groceries	80	0	20	0
Furniture	50	9	37	4
Farm machinery	42	0	38	20
Banking	76	0	24	0
Doctor	72	0	26	2
Lawyer	62	0	38	0
Dry cleaning	7	0	93	0
Hospital	0	23	70	7

Table 1.5.   Places in Which Anita Residents Shop

	Anita	Omaha-Council Bluffs	Atlantic	Other
	Percentage of Anita residents making last purchase in:			
Men's work clothes	78	0	11	11
Men's shoes	52	12	34	2
Men's suit	47	13	34	6
Children's clothes	32	22	28	18
Women's shoes	17	19	53	11
Women's coat	3	19	72	6
Teenage girls' clothes	0	0	40	60
Groceries	100	0	0	0
Drugs	97	0	3	0
Furniture	83	6	8	3
Banking	97	0	3	0
Doctor	89	0	11	0
Lawyer	80	0	17	3
Dry cleaning	3	3	91	3
Hospital	0	44	56	0

CHAPTER TWO

Systematic variations of the hierachy

In establishing that retail and service businesses cluster into orders based upon the sizes of market areas required for profitable operation, that market centers form levels based upon the economic reach provided by their centrality, and that the orders and levels interlock in a spatial system (the central-place hierarchy), we have only begun to develop a picture of the geography of retail and service business. There are many features of the system still to be remarked; how, for example, it varies from one part of the United States to another, and the manner in which it undergoes a change in form at high population densities within cities.

Variations in Market Areas

For any of the market areas presented in the preceding maps, we can calculate the total area served and the total population residing in that area. If these numbers are used to plot points in a graph, and it is noted whether the point refers to a village, town, small city, or regional capital, the scatter diagram shown in Figure 2.1 results. Since the graph has a logarithmic scale on both axes, straight lines drawn upward to the right at an angle of 45° trace out equal population densities (see Fig. 2.8 for the addition of the density scale).

First note in Figure 2.1 how the set of points slopes upward, tracing out the average level of density of southwestern Iowa. Distinct parts of the swarm are occupied by centers of each level, however, in lines of points inclined in excess of 45°. Larger lower-density trade areas are at the top of each line, and smaller higher-density areas are at the bottom. This pattern is created because rural population densities decline with distance from urban centers, and therefore the larger the trade area the lower the population density, other things being equal. Note how each

26

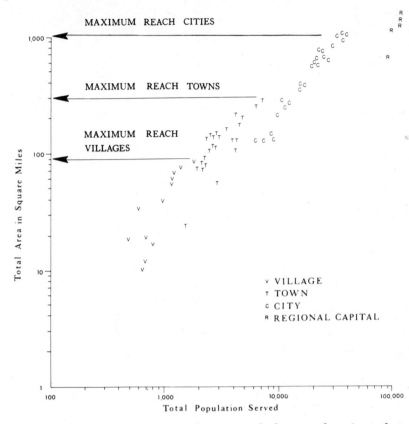

Fig. 2.1. *Scatter diagram: log of trade area graphed against log of population served shows the levels of the hierarchy.*

line has an upper limit of trade area size, defining objectively the maximum economic reach of center of its level.

Figure 2.2 adds another perspective. It repeats the scatter of points in Figure 2.1, but identifies the market areas of the lowest-order functions (such as groceries) of the villages, towns, and cities, the next order of activities (such as dry cleaning) provided by the towns, cities, and regional capital, and the highest order activities (such as clothing sales) provided only by the county seats and regional capital. The steplike pattern of Table 1.1 is re-emphasized, and thresholds of the different orders of activities can be seen. Further, the market areas of higher level centers are greater than those of lower level centers for the same order of goods.

This may also be noted in Figure 2.3, which shows, for farmers' trips to buy food and clothing, how the maximum distance consumers are willing to travel depends upon the level of the hierarchy, as measured by the number of *central functions* (i.e., the number of different *kinds* of retail and service business) provided. A dot is plotted for each con-

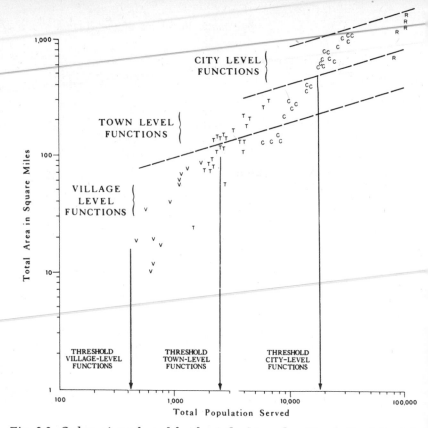

Fig. 2.2. *Orders of goods and levels of the hierarchy. Thresholds defined by factor analysis. (See reference in footnote 2, page 75.)*

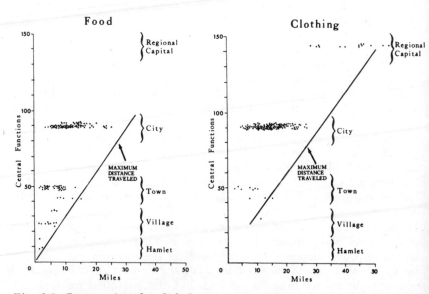

Fig. 2.3. *Ranges of food and clothing stores at different levels of the hierarchy.*

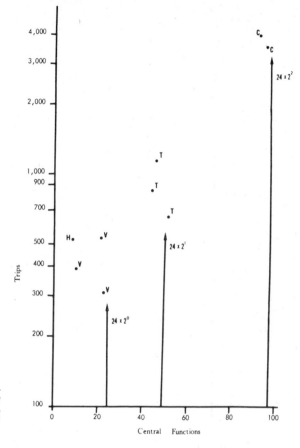

Fig. 2.4. *Relation between total inbound and outbound trips and size of center.*

sumer interviewed, identifying the size of center visited and the distance traveled.

Total consumer travel to and from the central places varies in a related way. Data are available for the point of origin and destination of automobiles traveling in the study area during an average summer day in 1960, as well as for the number of miles of travel involved.[1] Figures 2.4 and 2.5 summarize the evidence. Atlantic was the point of arrival for 1,912 trips and the point of departure for 1,994. The total vehicle-miles of travel involved were 46,900 and 44,600, respectively, or in excess of 90,000. For the town of Villisca the figures were: trips in, 433; out, 422; vehicle-miles in, 9,010; out, 8,490. For villages, inbound and outbound trips average 200, with perhaps 2,500 vehicle-miles of total travel each way. Note in both illustrations: (1) the approximate straight-line relationships between the trip variables and central functions, and (2) the clusters of points

[1] The data were assembled by the Iowa State Highway Commission as part of a 1960 statewide traffic assignment study (published as *Iowa Statewide Traffic Assignment: General Procedures*, 1964). The material used here is drawn from F. Wegmann's "Functional Rural Highway Classification and Central Places," an unpublished paper prepared at Northwestern University in March 1965.

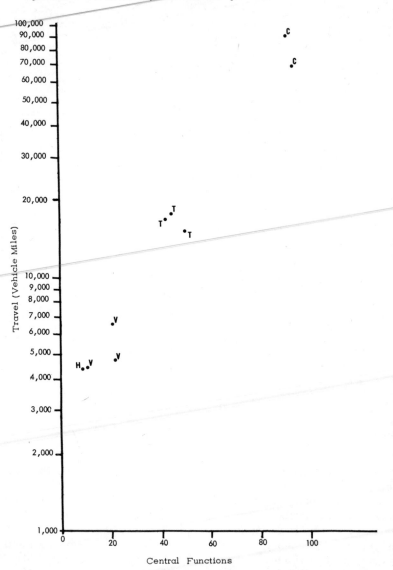

Fig. 2.5. *Relation between total vehicle-miles of travel and size of center.*

relating to the levels of the hierarchy. Use will be made later of the statement inserted on Figure 2.4, to the effect that the levels of the hierarchy
fall at approximately 24, 48, and 96 functions, or 24×2^0, 24×2^1, and
24×2^2.

The scope may now be enlarged to include the two study areas in South
Dakota (Figs. 2.6 and 2.7), and the central city and suburbs of Chicago
(Figure 2.20). Trade areas were obtained by field survey in each of
these areas and added to the Iowa pattern to produce Figure 2.8. Note
the systematic increase of trade area size with decreasing population

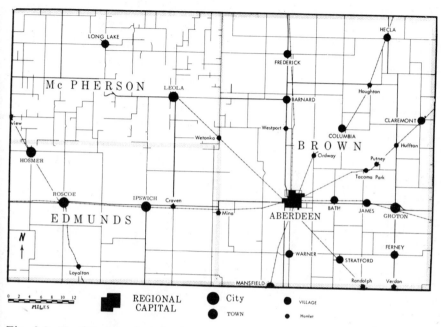

Fig. 2.6. Northeast South Dakota.

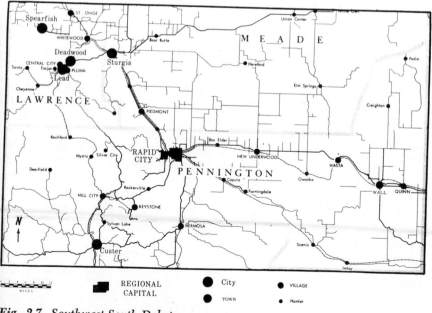

Fig. 2.7. Southwest South Dakota.

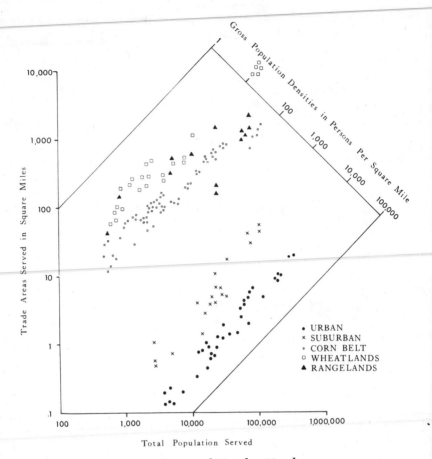

Fig. 2.8. *Trade areas expand as population densities drop.*

densities. The only irregularities are in southwestern South Dakota, which includes not only rangelands but also higher density mining and recreational areas in the Black Hills.

If the levels of the hierarchy are added, as in Figure 2.9, other important features emerge. First, the different levels of the central-place hierarchy in each of the rural areas and the levels of a hierarchy of business centers within cities are so consistent that straight lines may be drawn linking the upper limits of the points corresponding to similar levels under different conditions of population density. Corresponding to the differentiation of market centers into villages, towns, and cities in rural areas is a differentiation of urban shopping facilities into street-corner convenience clusters, neighborhood, community, and regional shopping centers.

If the effects of decreases in population density were simply to "stretch out" the central-place hierarchy in a consistent manner (if one could map the city pattern on rubber sheet, stretch it out, and call it

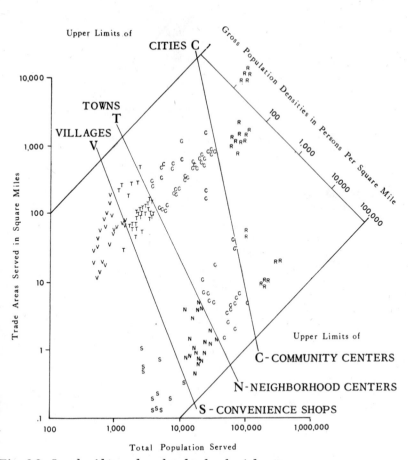

Fig. 2.9. *Levels of hierarchy related to levels of density.*

"Iowa"), Figure 2.9 would be less interesting than it is. The breaks between levels of centers would be vertical straight lines, keeping populations of the trade areas constant and allowing only square mile areas to increase or decrease proportionate with density shifts. But this is not so; all lines separating levels slope backward to the left, indicating that trade areas increase in size as densities drop, but not as fast as the densities decline, so that the sizes of populations served fall. Correspondingly, functions with the greatest threshold requirements at any level of the hierarchy move up to the next level. As a result, populations of central places fall because the *economic base* of the market towns has declined.

Figure 2.10 shows how the populations of centers at each level decline with densities, by numbers scaled along the lines marking upper limits of levels. Thus, towns drop from 1,600 to 400 population. Comparing the functions of centers in Iowa and South Dakota, we see that towns in the latter, at lower densities of population, can no longer provide the following businesses: furniture stores, appliance sales, variety stores, insurance

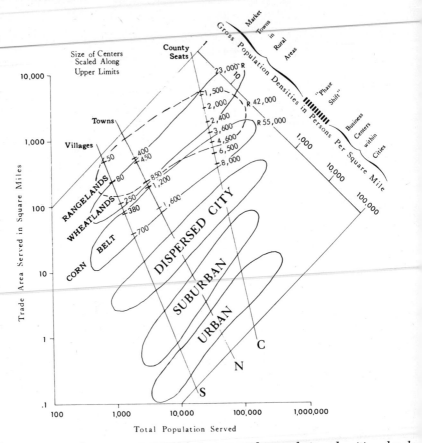

Fig. 2.10. *Trade area sizes, populations served, population densities, levels of the hierarchy, and populations of the market centers.*

and real estate brokers, movers and haulers, funeral homes, doctors, and dentists. Similarly, the simplest facilities of local government, farm implement dealers, and barber and beauty shops are no longer found in the villages, but have centralized to the towns.

The reason for this upward shift of functions to centers at higher levels of the hierarchy as population densities drop is as follows. To maintain a given array of activities, market areas must increase in size in direct proportion to the drop in population densities; the maximum distance consumers are willing to travel to the center must increase in similar proportion to the density decline. Evidently consumers are willing to travel further where densities are lower, for movement will generally be easier where people are fewer and congestion is less, so that the economic reach of centers does increase. The change is *less* than proportionate, however, so centers' functions must adjust to the declining numbers of consumers that can be reached within the trade areas of increasing radius. Similarly, at very high densities, congestion will not completely localize consumer movements, so that business centers of any given level within cities reach more consumers and are functionally more complex than their rural counterparts.

Correlates of Center Size

The foregoing implies that *if* the ranges of centers were to increase proportionately to the declines in density, centers would not have to adjust their functions. This suggests that there are some constant correlates of center size; for example, that a given number of consumers will be served by a given mix and number of retail establishments. Figures 2.11 to 2.13 illustrate this point in rural cases. The resident population, number of business types, and number of establishments of each center have been graphed against one another. The idea of Figure 2.11 is that the population of centers is dependent upon the number of different kinds of business that they provide to their market areas; the correlation is 0.95. Note how the different study areas display the same pattern.

A few centers deviate, however, such as Lead in the Black Hills and Glenwood in Iowa. These centers perform *specialized functions* in addition to their role as market centers, so their resident populations are inflated without any corresponding increases in size of market area. Lead is a mining center, and Glenwood has a state mental institution. If the 1,800 residents of that institution were subtracted from Glenwood's reported population in Figure 2.11, the center would have almost exactly the population which might be predicted from its retail and service offerings.

Central-place principles provide a complete statement of urban location only when urban centers are supported exclusively as market centers by the retail and service functions they provide for surrounding regions. Wide deviations in urban population from that predicted by an understanding of the geography of retail and service business will result if a center has specialized functions. These functions may be related to the geography of production, for example, if one is dealing with a mining town in a region of primary production, a factory town in the manufacturing belt, a railroad town at a classification yard, or a port. Specialized functions support a residential population, which in turn supports retail and service activities within the town. But the retail and service provision so supported is less than in a market center of similar population size because the resident population is not matched by the residents of a corresponding rural region.

A similar situation exists if a center is drawn within commuting radius of the metropolis, into what the economists call the metropolitan labor market and the geographers and sociologists call the metropolitan region. Such a center would probably become a commuting suburb. Again, it would have a higher population than might be predictable from the retail activities located in it, as with the Seattle suburbs in northern Snohomish County identified by an S in Figure 2.13.

Figure 2.12 shows, for the Iowa case, how total population within the

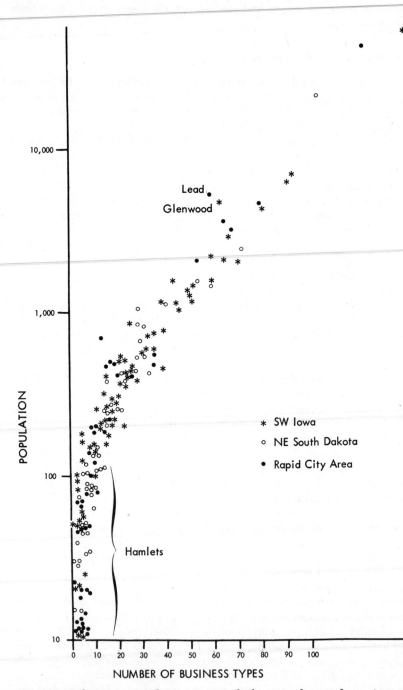

Fig. 2.11. *Relation of population of central places to the numbers of types of business performed.*

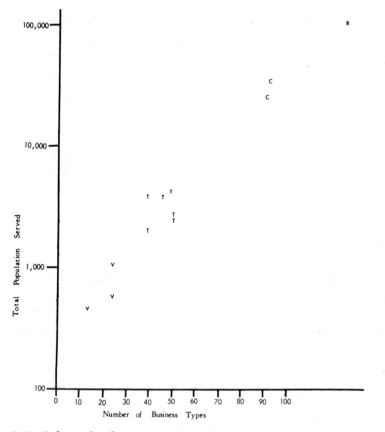

Fig. 2.12. *Relationship between total population served and numbers of types of business performed.*

maximum economic reach of centers varies with the functions performed by those centers, re-emphasizing the regularity of the progression.

The idea of Figure 2.11 is that the population of a central place is dependent upon the total number of *kinds* of retail and service business offered. This number, in turn, in part depends upon and in part determines the centrality and economic reach of the center. Therefore, Figure 2.13 states that the total *number* of retail and service establishments located in a center is a function of center population, recognizing that a center's population, while supported by the central-place functions, also places demands upon those functions as it seeks to supply its own needs. The responses will be varied. Some stores will just grow in size, others will duplicate identical units, yet others will begin to specialize. In any case, Figure 2.13 shows the rate of growth of establishments to be proportional to the rate of growth of center population (the graph is double logarithmic, so that straight lines depict constant rates); because both center population and total population served are related in the same manner to types of business (Figs. 2.11 and 2.12), the rate of growth

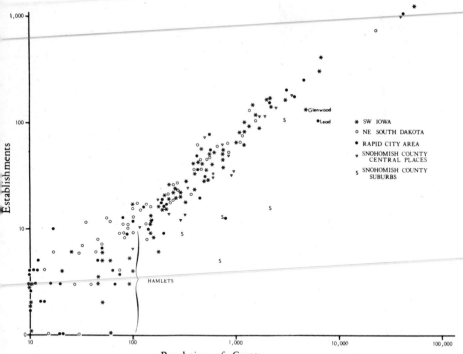

Fig. 2.13. *Relation of total retail and service establishments to center population.*

of establishments is also proportional to growth of total population served.

In Figure 2.4 it was noted that the progression of central functions in the villages, towns, and cities of Iowa was approximately 24, 48, and 96, but that this could also be written as 24×2^0, 24×2^1, and 24×2^2, where the 0, 1, and 2 exponents describe the order of centers in the hierarchy less 1, beginning with order 1 for the villages and proceeding upward. See Figure 2.14 (to introduce a term used in some of the literature, this figure uses "functional units" instead of 'establishments').

The Aberdeen region of South Dakota displays a similar progression of types: approximately 15, 30, and 60, or 15×2^0, 15×2^1, and 15×2^2. It appears that a general expression for the progression of business types at the different levels of the hierarchy is $d2^{w-1}$, where w is the order of the hierarchy and d is a number that varies from area to area. Since we have already noted the "slippage" of the functions of centers as population densities drop, we must conclude that d varies with population densities, indicating that businesses present at lower levels of the hierarchy have moved up to the next level of the hierarchy in areas with lower densities.[2]

[2] I am indebted to Michael Woldenberg for pointing out the $d2^{w-1}$ relationship to me, and comparing it to the concepts of stream order and the bifurcation ratio in river systems.

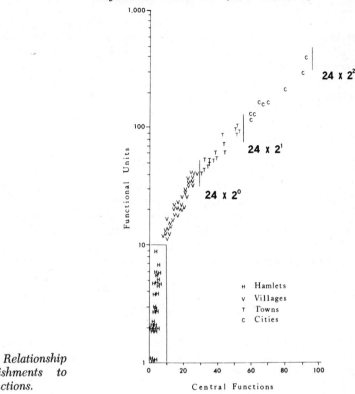

Fig. 2.14. *Relationship of establishments to central functions.*

If d varies with density, what is the significance of the number 2 that appears in the equation? It stems from the spatial pattern of centers in the hierarchy. This is illustrated in Figure 2.15. Along the main transport routes, from east to west, the sequence of centers is: city, village, town, village, city . . . . This pattern repeats itself between cities in a north-south direction. Each city thus has surrounding it a ring of four towns, and each town also lies on the ring of one other city. On the average, there are two towns for every city. Similarly, each town and city has a ring of four villages, and every village lies at the midpoint between a town and a city. For every town and city there are, on the average, two villages. The ratio of lower-level centers to centers of the next highest level is two. The *bifurcation ratio* is, therefore, two.

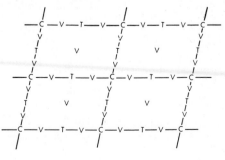

Fig. 2.15. *The rhomboidal spatial pattern of central places in Iowa.*

Iowa's settlement pattern is rectilinear or rhomboidal, a result of the rectangular land use survey and the manner in which the railroads were built; the successive doubling of lower-level centers, located at midpoints between higher order places, is to be expected. In its most general form the equation we have been examining should be dk^{w-1}. This relates the bifurcation ratio k, the order of the hierarchy w, and the effects of population density, as expressed in d.

Laws of Retail Gravitation

Knowing the population and central functions of each center and distances between centers, market areas can be determined without undertaking extensive and expensive consumer surveys.

In one of the earliest contributions to marketing science, William J. Reilly developed his *laws of retail gravitation* to summarize market area patterns. His "breaking-point" equation,[3] states that the trade area boundary between two towns, A and B, is, in miles from B, equal to:

$$\frac{\text{Miles between A and B}}{1 + \sqrt{\dfrac{\text{Size of A}}{\text{Size of B}}}}$$

In most applications, Reilly used population as an index of size, but number of central functions can be used, since it is a fundamental measure of the attractiveness of a center. Thus between Atlantic (A) and Red Oak (B), we compute:

$$d_{AB} = 36 \text{ miles}$$
$$S_A = 92 \text{ types of business}$$
$$S_B = 90 \text{ types of business}$$

and therefore the distance from Red Oak to the market area breaking point is

$$\frac{36}{1 + \sqrt{\dfrac{92}{90}}}$$

---

[3] William J. Reilly, *The Law of Retail Gravitation* (New York: Reilly, 1931); Paul D. Converse, "Development of Marketing: Fifty Years of Progress," in H. G. Wales, ed., *Changing Perspectives in Marketing* (Urbana: Univ. of Illinois, 1951); George Schwartz, *Development of Marketing Theory* (Chicago: South-Western, 1963). A related statement is Fetter's "law of market areas," if we substitute "attractiveness" or size of center for market prices and distances for freight rates: "The boundary line between the territories tributary to two geographically competing markets for like goods is a hyberbolic curve. At each point on the curve the difference between freights from two markets is just equal to the difference between the prevailing market prices, whereas on either side of the line the freight difference and price difference are unequal. The relation of prices in the two markets determines the location of the boundary line: the lower the price in a market relative to that of a neighboring market, the larger the tributary territory." Frank A. Fetter, "The Economic Law of Market Areas," *Quarterly Journal of Economics*, Vol. 38 (1924), 520–29. See also C. D. and W. P. Hyson, "The Economic Law of Market Areas," *Quarterly Journal of Economics*, Vol. 64 (1959), 319–27.

or 17.8 miles, which is two miles south of Griswold by road. Look back to Figure 1.13 to see how close this is to actual farmer preferences.

The equation cannot be applied indiscriminately. It must be applied only to cities and larger regional centers to develop market areas for goods of city order. Towns may be added to derive market areas for the next lower order of goods, and villages to see how the lowest order of function can "squeeze in." In rural areas the breaking-point formula works quite well if applied in this way (which differs in spirit from Reilly's usage), because of the interdependence of distance and size of center as the opposing forces of attraction and impedance affecting consumer choice. If alternatives are the same, consumers will choose the closest center, but the breaking-point will always be deflected at the outer margin towards the less attractive of two alternatives.

The neat breaking-point vanishes at higher population densities. In rural areas distance has a major impact on choice because the time and cost involved in traveling to a center are so great. On one side of a breaking-point the farmers all travel in one direction; on the other side they travel to the other center. Differences in attractiveness of centers simply serve to pull the breaking-point one way or another.

Within metropolitan regions, however, there is no such thing as an absolute breaking-point. The breaking-point formula simply gives the point at which the proportion of consumers located around the breaking-point splits equally between two competing alternatives of differing attractiveness. Reilly's original law of retail gravitation becomes relevant: "Two centers attract trade from intermediate places approximately in direct proportion to the sizes of the centers and in inverse proportion to the square of the distances from these two centers to the intermediate place," or:

$$\frac{T_A}{T_B} = \frac{P_A}{P_B}\left(\frac{D_B}{D_A}\right)^2$$

where

T_A, T_B = proportions of trade from the intermediate place attracted by centers A and B

P_A, P_B = sizes of A and B

D_A, D_B = distances of A and B from the intermediate place

This model is deterministic; it says that T_A/T_B is exactly the proportion of trade that will move in one direction or another. Yet it is known that within a city *individual* behavior is probabilistic. Deterministic approaches remain relevant in rural areas, where choice is severely constrained by distance and the number of alternatives is restricted. However, in densely built-up areas consumers have considerable business centers of differing attractiveness available within the maximum distances they are willing to travel. They will visit none exclusively, but each at some time and with some probability. One probability model, developed by

Huff in the Reilly tradition, appears to work well.[4] Where p_{A1} is the probability that a consumer located at A will visit center 1, and there are r differing shopping opportunities of sizes $S_1 \ldots S_r$ located at travel times $T_{A1} \ldots T_{Ar}$ from A, the model is

$$p_{A1} = \frac{\dfrac{S_1}{T_{A1}^{\alpha}}}{\displaystyle\sum_{i=1}^{r} \dfrac{S_i}{T_{Ai}^{\alpha}}}$$

and of course $\sum_i p_{Ai} = 1.0$. α is a parameter which varies for different levels of the hierarchy. Applying this model to a variety of residential areas will result in a set of probabilities of visiting each center for each area. Probability contours can be drawn for any center, linking areas which have the same probability of being visited. The equivalent of the traditional market area boundary between any pair of centers is the point at which contours of similar value are tangential. Figure 2.16 shows three places where only two-way choices are made, so the points of indifference are the tangents of the 0.5 probability contours. A third indifference point is the meeting of the 0.33 contours from each of the three centers; there one finds equality of the three-way interaction probabilities.

The Urban Case

Figure 2.10 shows that the hierarchy of business centers within cities is consistently related to the hierarchy of market centers in rural areas. The expectation is that, because of higher population densities within cities, centers of comparable level in the hierarchy will be functionally more complex than their rural counterparts.

The urban case differs in significant ways from the rural, however, and the differences increase with size of center. The functions performed by a village in Iowa will group somewhat loosely in a single business area, although a gas station, bulk fuel oil depot, or church may be located on the outskirts of the settlement. An Iowa town has a much better-defined central business core, and may have several additional clusters of business on the main highways at the edges of town, one or more of them catering to highway traffic. Others may include services that demand more space than can be afforded in the central business area, such as lumber yards. Small cities like Atlantic have definite central business districts (CBD's) in which the highest-threshold functions they provide locate. Within these CBD's there is structure and pattern, for the different kinds of business sort themselves out according to the amounts they are willing to pay for the most central location, the main highway intersection. Each CBD is therefore characterized by a cone of

---

[4] David L. Huff, "A Probability Analysis of Shopping Center Trading Areas," *Land Economics*, Vol. 53 (February 1963), 81–90, based on R. Duncan Luce, *Individual Choice Behavior* (New York: Wiley, 1958). Huff, *Determination of Intra-Urban Retail Trade Areas* (Los Angeles: Univ. of California Real Estate Research Program, 1962).

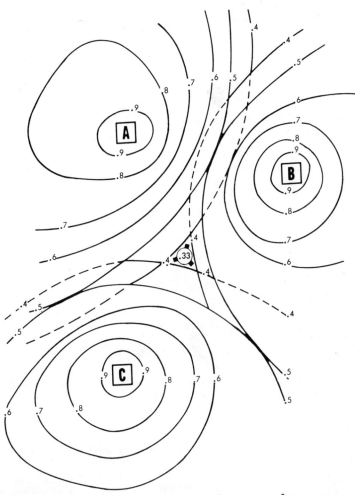

Fig. 2.16. *Probability contours for consumers shopping in three centers.*

land value which is highest at the main intersection and declines away from it. In addition, the small cities have peripheral highway-oriented business strips of restaurants, motels, and gas stations, and business "ribbons" along which are located the space-consuming businesses which cannot afford CBD sites, and service businesses such as plumbing and electrical companies, who do not need them. The population of these small cities has grown large enough to make it profitable for enterprising businessmen to locate in the several residential neighborhoods and to supply them with goods and services, in competition with the CBD, of the order provided by villages to farmers. The small cities show the first explicit emergence of a hierarchy of business centers *within* the urban area.

Figure 2.17 gives some indication of how the number of separate business areas varies with size of center in Iowa. In this diagram, a business

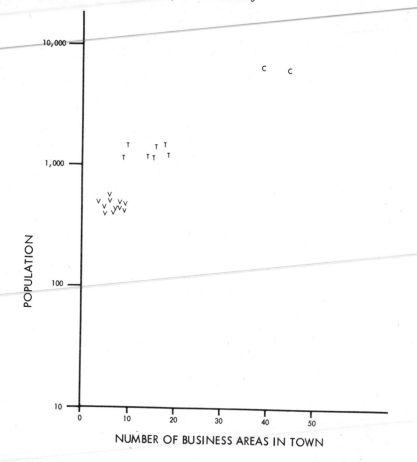

Fig. 2.17. *Relationship between number of business areas within town and the population of central places in Iowa.*

area is defined as a group of contiguous business establishments, or as a single store located beyond reasonable walking distance of another store.

From the county seat level the complexity of business structure within cities increases. The regional cities have larger and more complex highway-oriented strips and business ribbons, and further types of specialized business areas. In addition, their regional functions are provided from the CBD, but the urban residents obtain lower-order goods from outlying business centers of at least two levels.

This successive elaboration culminates within a major metropolis like Chicago, in which seven million people spread across nine counties in two states. The over-all pattern of consumer-orientation of business land use remains (Figure 2.18—shaded areas indicate non-residential land). However, the structure of business areas has become incredibly complex, as the typology in Figure 2.19 indicates, comprising:

(1) *A hierarchy of business centers.* Functions such as grocery stores, drug stores, barber shops, variety and clothing stores, and department

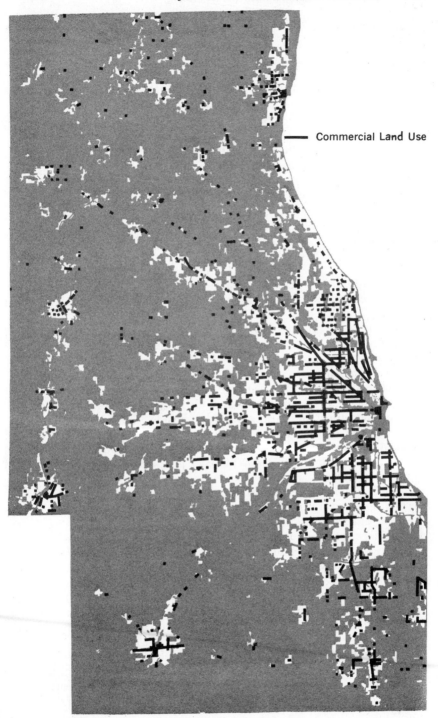

Commercial Land Use

Fig. 2.18. Business land use: Chicago metropolitan area.

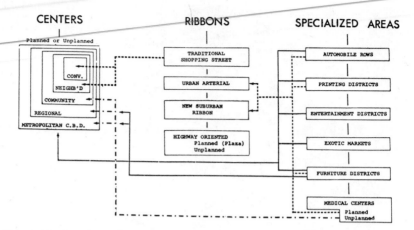

Fig. 2.19. *Typology of business areas within the metropolis.*

stores locate here. There is pressure for the various functions to cluster because customers tend to shop from store to store during a given shopping trip.

(2) *Highway-oriented ribbons.* These are composed of service stations, restaurants, and motels, and they serve demands originating on the highways.

(3) *Urban arterial commercial developments.* Most of the functions located on arterials like reasonable access to the urban market, but because of space requirements and the ways in which consumers use them, they function most efficiently outside the nucleated business centers. The establishments in this group are usually associated with special single-purpose trips; examples are furniture and appliance stores, automobile repair shops, radio-TV sales and service establishments, and plumbing shops.

(4) *Specialized functional areas.* These areas are characterized by the presence of several related types of establishments, notably dealerships in new and used cars in "automobile rows," and doctors, dentists, X-ray technicians, and so forth in medical complexes. Such functional areas are held intact by close linkages provided by comparative shopping, economies in advertising in the case of automobile dealers, and referrals and common use of specialists and special services in the case of medical districts. Most such functional areas require easy accessibility to that segment of the urban market required for their support.

Even this typology fails to capture the real diversity, because conventional classifications of business types break down within the metropolis. One cannot speak simply of an automobile repair garage, but must consider explicitly the range of repair services provided. This range increases, as does the specialization of shops in different parts of the range, as city size increases.[5] This is equally true for most kinds of busi-

[5] Otis Dudley Duncan, "Service Industries and the Urban Hierarchy," *Papers and Proceedings of the Regional Science Association*, Vol. 5 (1959), 105–20.

ness. Within the metropolis, scales of business establishments and the multiple shades of specialization of each must be recognized at the outset.

Chicago's business pattern is typical of American metropolitan areas. It developed in response to the spread of commuting suburbs across counties in which business was originally provided by a hierarchy of rural market centers and a string of river towns in which grist mills had been built. Twelve railroads were constructed radiating from Chicago's "Loop," the metropolitan CBD; after they gained access to Loop terminals in the early twentieth century they enabled a finger-like rail-commuting suburban development pattern to crystallize. The character was simple: a large central city with 12 radii along which suburbs strung like beads, determined by station locations, out to a distance of 30 miles. Beyond these suburbs was a discontinuous crescent of relatively independent industrial satellites: Waukegan, Elgin, Aurora, Joliet, Chicago Heights, and, in Indiana, steel-making towns like Gary. The metropolis ended at this crescent, as it does today. Beyond is open farmland, and a central-place hierarchy of county seats, towns, and villages.

Within the satellite crescent, each of the railroad axes consisted of a succession of higher-density developments around the railroad stations, lower-density developments along the axes between the stations, and large areas of open space between the radii (Fig. 2.20). Each of the radii tended to have towns similar in the socio-economic status of their residents. Crossing the radii in bands encircling the central city, towns at similar distances from the CBD tended to have similar mixtures of housing types, with those at greater distances being of lower density, with larger lots and fewer apartments. In addition, the kinds of families (in terms of size, stage in the life cycle, and life-style) tended to be similar in the same band. Thus, each small zone of the metropolitan area, comprising towns on a given radial within the same distance band, could be thought a "community" of residents with similar income characteristics and life-style. The local business center, located by the railroad station, reflected this similarity.[6]

Much of this socio-economic symmetry remains today as the underpinning of Chicago's business pattern. As Figures 2.18 and 2.20 indicate, consumer orientation of business has led to a system that criss-crosses the continuously built-up central city, following the section and half-section streets and the spines of the radii. A complete hierarchy of business centers can be identified, from street-corner clusters of convenience shops, through neighborhood, community, and regional shopping centers, and culminating in the Loop, the metropolitan CBD.

In 1958 the Loop had over 2,000 retail stores employing more than 46,000 persons, and sales of $700 million. The largest outlying regional shopping centers within the city of Chicago each had approximately 250 establishments of more than 70 different kinds employing over 4,000 people, sales of almost $90 million, more than 8,000 front feet of space,

[6] We might note that the classic theories of urban sociology and ecology, urban geography, and economics were based upon this symmetry, as it was revealed by social scientists at the University of Chicago in their studies during the 1920's and 1930's.

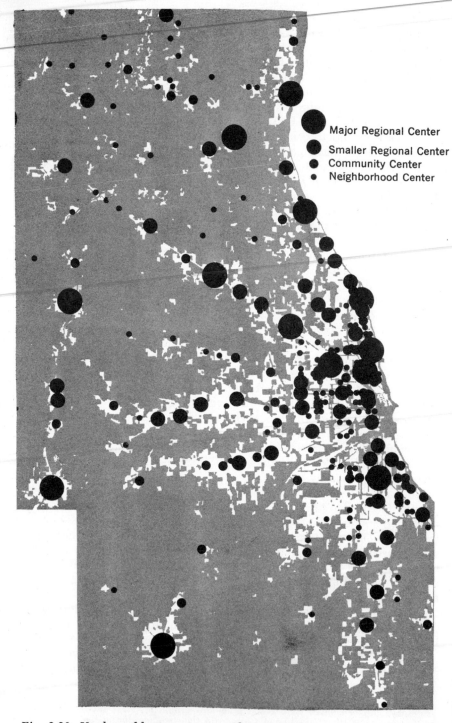

Fig. 2.20. *Unplanned business centers: Chicago region.*

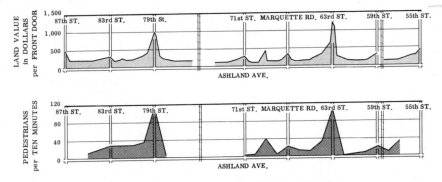

Fig. 2.21. *Land values and pedestrian counts along Ashland Avenue.*

and a ground floor area of 800,000 square feet. More than 27,000 trips were made to such centers on an average shopping day. The shopping-goods trade area of one such center within the central city was 15.5 square miles, reaching 350,000 people with an aggregate income exceeding $800 million, although its convenience-goods trade area was only 2.1 square miles, reaching 70,000 people with an aggregate income of $90 million. Similarly, community shopping centers had 70 stores of some 36 types, over 100,000 square feet of floor area, 500 employees, and sales of $13 million; they attracted 10,000 trips daily and reached a trade area of 40,000 to 50,000 people within the 2 to 3 adjacent square miles.[7]

Suburban centers had similar characteristics. Regional centers performed 80 different functions in 300 establishments, with total center areas of one million square feet (over 500,000 square feet of ground floor area). Trade areas reached 100,000 people. For community centers, comparable data are 40 types and 80 establishments; 400,000 square feet total center area and 200,000 square feet establishment ground floor area; 40,000 to 50,000 people reached. The reason suburban centers have more functions than city centers is that lawyers, accountants, and similar professionals within the city congregate in the Loop, whereas at greater distances from the city center the suburbs are able to retain them locally.

Minute differences in location within centers make a great deal of difference to sales volumes because of differences in pedestrian traffic, so the retail businesses that cluster in centers compete vigorously to occupy the best possible sites. One result is shown in Figure 2.21. Along Ashland Avenue in Chicago there are two main business intersections, at 63rd Street and 79th Street. The number of pedestrians drops off sharply from these intersections, so it is essential for retail businesses to have sites as close to the intersections as possible. Competition for these sites leads to an increase in their land values; the desirability of sites for business location, as mirrored in what businessmen are willing to pay for the land, replicates the pattern of consumers walking along the street.

----

[7] Complete data for Chicago's business centers will be found in Berry and Robert J. Tennant, *Chicago Commercial Reference Handbook* (Department of Geography Research Paper No. 86, Univ. of Chicago, 1963). For comparison see Eileen Schell, *Changes in Boston's Retail Landscape* (New York: Retail Research Institute, 1964).

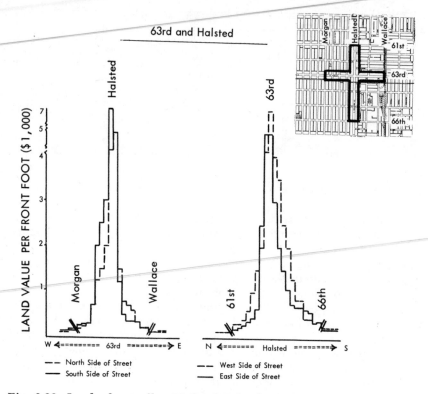

Fig. 2.22. *Land value profiles: 63rd and Halsted center.*

The land-value profiles for the 63rd and Halsted business center in Chicago are shown in Figure 2.22. In this biggest of Chicago's older outlying centers, values at the peak reach $7,000 per front foot (they exceed $40,000 per front foot at State and Madison Streets, the central intersection, or "100 per cent location," of the Loop), and drop to $250 per front foot at the edge. Lines indicate how the center may be delineated on the basis of land values, to separate it from surrounding ribbon business uses. With such wide differences in values within centers, uses sort themselves out on the basis of need and ability to pay for the most central spot. The succession of uses, with distance from the principal intersection of a regional center in Chicago, is: [8] (1) at the core: apparel accessories, hosiery, candy, department stores, shoes, clothes, drugs, jewelry, corsets and lingerie, and other miscellaneous clothing; (2) in the next zone: household appliances, bakeries, currency exchange, motion picture theaters, delicatessens, restaurants, banks, radio and television sales, loans, millinery, optometrists, gifts, cameras, insurance offices, watch repair; (3) at the periphery: hardware, furniture, groceries, meats, liquor, sporting goods, medical services, photographers, real estate offices, china

[8] Barry J. Garner, *The Internal Structure of Retail Nucleations*, Northwestern Studies in Geography, XII (Evanston, 1966).

and glassware, draperies, music, barber and beauty shops, laundromats, and floor coverings.

The distinction is clear. Regional functions of highest threshold are at the core, together with those uses whose sales are critically affected by pedestrian volume (candy stores, women's hosiery, and so on). At the periphery are personal service establishments of neighborhood level. The intermediate zone contains a mixture of regional and community level uses. Rent differences have forced large space-consumers such as furniture stores to the periphery.

In community centers, the regional level core is, of course, eliminated, and the core contains community-order functions, with a periphery of those of neighborhood level.

Therefore, the rent-paying ability of uses appears to be affected predominantly by their order in the hierarchy, and the internal zoning of uses within business centers mirrors the level at which these functions appear in the hierarchy. The highest-order use in a center is usually that use needing and able to pay for the most central location within it.

The central business district of any major metropolis has a marked and distinctive spatial structure. An initial distinction may be made between the "core" and the "frame" of the CBD. The frame, a concentric zone around the core, includes downtown manufacturing and areas devoted to wholesaling and warehousing, although new freeways have led to the decentralization of these services. The core contains the retail district (the most central of all central places in the geography of retailing) clustered around the "100 per cent location" of maximum pedestrian densities and land values; separate office districts devoted to finance, insurance, medical services, and the like; one or more entertainment districts; clusters of hotels; and areas of downtown apartments. Scattered throughout are different kinds of more local retail uses. The main retail district pulls in consumers from the entire metropolitan area, although it relies to an increasing extent upon the trade of workers in downtown offices and apartments. The entertainment district has its own peculiar assemblage of retail uses and services. Office buildings have restaurants, gift shops, barber and beauty shops, and stores offering a range of clothing and lingerie for office girls. The apartment clusters each have neighborhood services, the nature of these varying markedly from expensive high-rise developments to depressed apartment hotels of "skid row." [9] Figure 2.23 maps the functional areas within Chicago's central business district, the Loop.

In addition to the hierarchy of outlying business centers, with internal banding of uses, and the internal complexities of the CBD at the top of the hierarchy, the business structure of the metropolis includes business ribbons and a variety of specialized functional areas (Fig. 2.19). In addition to the kinds of ribbons noted earlier are: (1) strings of highway-oriented establishments; (2) arterial developments in which are found

[9] Ronald R. Boyce and Edgar M. Horwood, *Studies of the Central Business District and Urban Freeway Development* (Seattle: Univ. of Washington, 1959); Raymond E. Murphy, James E. Vance, and Bart J. Epstein, "Internal Structure of the C.B.D.," *Economic Geography*, Vol. 31 (January 1955), 21–46.

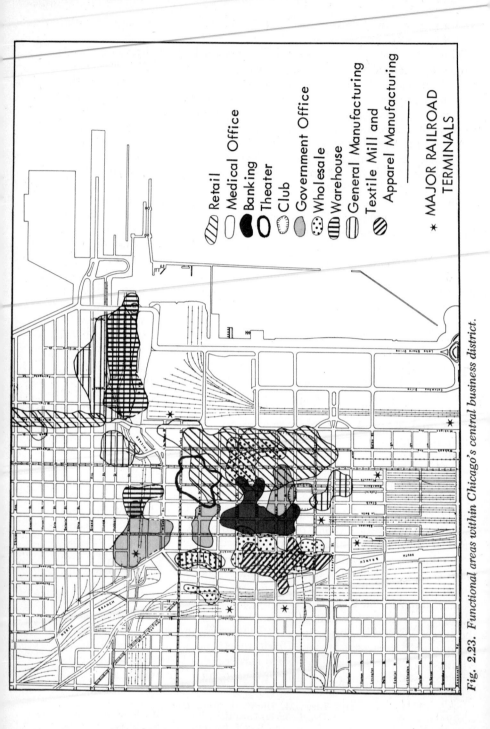

Legend:
- Retail
- Medical Office
- Banking
- Theater
- Club
- Government Office
- Wholesale
- Warehouse
- General Manufacturing
- Textile Mill and Apparel Manufacturing
- ★ MAJOR RAILROAD TERMINALS

Fig. 2.23. Functional areas within Chicago's central business district.

uses demanding too much space to be able to afford locations in centers; (3) retail and service uses needing only generally accessible location, not centrality to pedestrians, because the businessman is called to the home to perform his service (as in the case of a plumber or television repairman), or because the consumer makes a special single-purpose trip to the store for what it offers. Other kinds can also be found. One feature of the old central city was the ethnic diversity of its residential neighborhoods. Each of the traditional *neighborhood shopping streets* had its own flavor, be it Jewish, Italian, German, Czech, Chinese, Japanese, or Greek. Today only a few of these remain, for the older ethnic differences have gone, although the Negro shopping streets do develop some special character.[10]

Specialized functional areas develop because many kinds of uses *agglomerate* inside the largest cities to facilitate comparison buying, to serve a special market, or to make joint use of specialized facilities. Such clusters include automobile rows, furniture districts, and medical centers. Traditionally, professional offices were found in the CBD, or occupying upper floors in outlying business centers. Today, special buildings are constructed for them, often in clusters, providing joint access to laboratories and to services for which they have a common need.

To this diversity of business centers the postwar years have brought further complexity. The patterns illustrated in Figures 2.18 to 2.22 developed before the depression of the 1930's, and were crystallized by it and the succeeding wartime years.

Once the war was over, suburbanization accelerated, a development facilitated by the general ownership of automobiles and promoted by government loans for single-family housing. Part of the sprawl conformed to the older radial pattern, and made use of the railroads. But as new highways were built, suburbs spread into the inner interstices between the fingerlike radii, creating suburbs of increasing diversity that clouded the earlier socio-economic symmetry of the radii and rings.

At the same time came accelerated technological change in retailing, making use of the automobile; the unit of development changed from the single store to the entire *planned shopping plaza*. Figure 2.24 gives some idea of the results. The traditional pattern of centers remains, but major planned shopping plazas are now located in the interstices between and at the outer edges of the prewar built-up area.

Before World War II, the unplanned centers competed only with their nearest neighbors. If they were located in the central city, their trade areas overlapped with those of four or six neighbors, for densities were so high that several centers could survive within the maximum distances consumers were willing to travel. Along the radii, competition was with the next center towards the city and the next away from it. Thus these consumers, in contrast to those in rural areas, did not make deterministic choices on either side of a trade area boundary. A variety of alternatives

[10] Allan Pred, "Business Thoroughfares as Expression of Urban Negro Culture," *Economic Geography,* Vol. 39 (July 1963), 217–33.

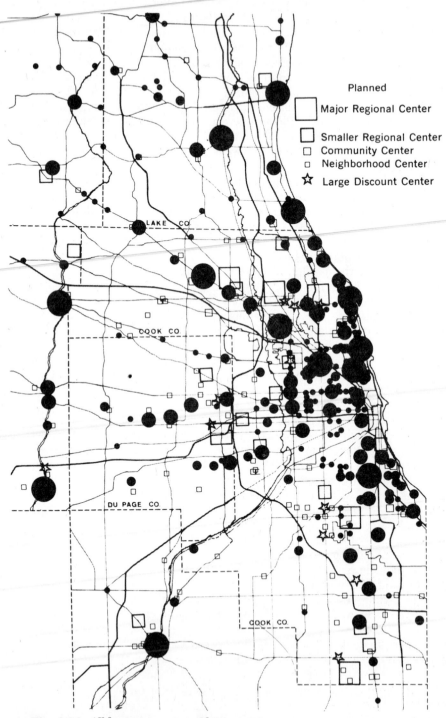

Fig. 2.24. *All business centers: Chicago region.*

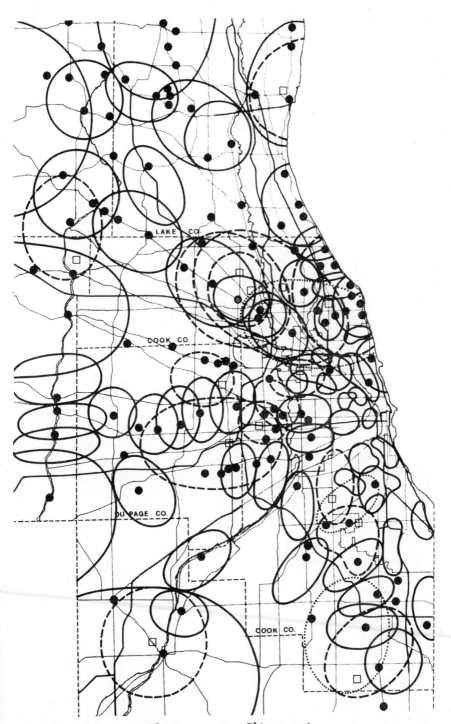

Fig. 2.25. *Market areas of business centers: Chicago region.*

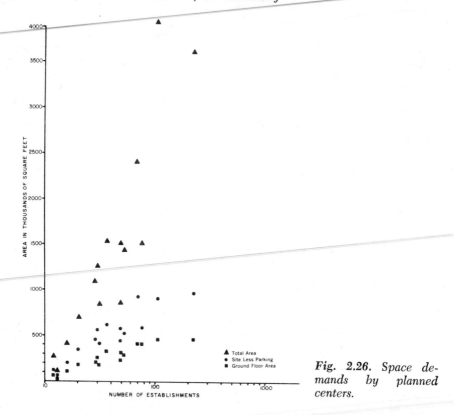

Fig. 2.26. Space de-
mands by planned
centers.

existed, and individual behavior could best be described as probabilistic in the sense of Huff's model.

The effect of planned centers has been to increase the range of choice and intensity of competition in the postwar period, as shown in Figure 2.25, which maps the areas from which centers draw consumers (but not the probability contours of each).

Once again there is a hierarchy. The new planned centers have the same number of levels as the older, unplanned developments, but they differ in many other respects. The unplanned centers are clusters of individually owned and built establishments, located by competition for central sites, and strung along the sides of streets away from a major intersection, with on-street parking and through traffic disturbing pedestrian movements. Planned centers are, conversely, complete developments located adjacent to, but not athwart, major highway intersections. Business establishments are located in an island amid surrounding parking lots, and carefully arranged along pedestrian walkways and around malls to give maximum exposure of all stores to consumers. Whereas the main attractions of unplanned centers are at the central intersection and other uses drop off from that point according to ability to pay, shopping plaza developers place the major attractions at opposite ends of the walkways, and string the other uses between. This arrangement is encouraged by the way in which major centers are financed. A developer

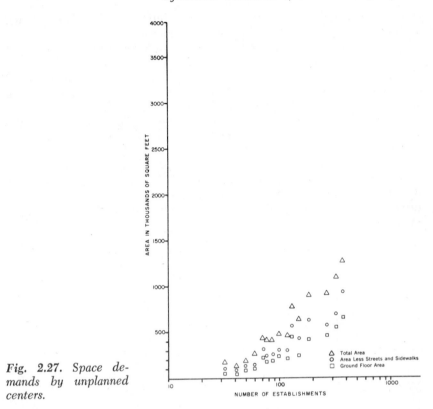

Fig. 2.27. Space demands by unplanned centers.

will persuade prospective major "triple-A" tenants to join him in developing a shopping center, and in return will give them rent concessions. Since they have triple-A business ratings, he is able to borrow money to construct the center. He makes his profits out of the smaller establishments attracted by the possibilities of maximum consumer exposure on the walkways connecting the major tenants, whose job, as far as the developer is concerned, is to draw consumers to the center.

The same regularities that characterized central places in Iowa and South Dakota also appear to be characteristic of both new planned shopping centers and old unplanned business districts in Chicago. Figures 2.26 and 2.27 contrast the space demands of the two kinds of centers and point up technological differences between the pre- and postwar types of business center design, however.

The "Phase Shift"

Figure 2.10 (page 34) identifies systematic relations between trade areas and population served, levels of the hierarchy, and population densities. The regularity applies at low densities to market centers and surrounding rural areas, but at high densities only to business centers within cities. The same ingredients are present at the two extremes, but because of the differences in densities there are two "states"; as with a mineral under pressure there is a "phase shift." At what densities and under what conditions does this shift take place?

The concept of the *dispersed city* is used to identify the beginnings of the phase shift. The idea is simple. Clusters of urban places exist with distances between them short enough for consumers to consider several within their range of alternative choice for shopping. Such places perform local functions for their own populations, but specialize in the performance of high-order functions for the group. One will become the automobile sales center, another the furniture center, another the medical center, and so forth.

When groups of places which appear to function as dispersed cities are examined in the United States, it is found that their average levels of density place them exactly between the intensive corn belt and the suburban cases of Figure 2.10—exactly where the phase shift is predicted to occur.[11]

---

[11] Ian Burton, "A Restatement of the Dispersed City Hypothesis," *Annals,* Association of American Geographers, Vol. 56 (September 1963), 285–89.

CHAPTER THREE

Classical central-place theory

Regularities in facts are plain to see. For a scientific understanding of the geography of retail and service business, it is necessary to predict these regularities from a theory. Ideally, a theory should embody a minimum of assumptions and postulates and produce the regularities as logical deductions. Only with such convergence of theory and fact can it be said that a science exists.

The bases of central-place theory were laid before World War II by two German scholars, geographer Walter Christaller and economist August Lösch, although certain of their conclusions were anticipated by American rural sociologist C. J. Galpin, and many earlier scholars, such as Leon Lalanne, stated at least the germ of their idea.[1] In Christaller much of the underlying theory is implicit, and it was Lösch who, in an independent derivation, made it explicit. In each case, the theory is developed essentially detached from considerations of the behavior of retailers and consumers over time and in space.

Both theorists agree on the spatial arrangement of stores required for optimal distribution of a single good to a dispersed population. However, their arguments diverge significantly when they seek to obtain locations for many kinds of goods considered simultaneously, with results that make Lösch's "economic landscapes" more relevant to secondary produc-

[1] Walter Christaller, *Die zentralen Orte in Süddeutschland* (Jena: Fischer, 1933); August Lösch, *Die räumliche Ordnung der Wirtschaft* (Jena: Fischer, 1940); C. J. Galpin, *The Social Anatomy of an Agricultural Community*, Research Bulletin 34, Agricultural Experiment Station of Univ. of Wisconsin, May 1915. Christaller's book is now available in a translation by C. Baskin: *The Central Places of Southern Germany* (Englewood Cliffs: Prentice-Hall, 1966). Lösch was translated by W. H. Woglom and W. F. Stolper as *The Economics of Location* (New Haven: Yale Univ., 1954). Leon Lalanne, "An Essay on the Theory of Railway Systems, Based on Observation of Facts and the Basic Laws Governing Population Distribution," *Comptes Rendus des Séances de l'Académie des Sciences*, Vol. 57 (1863), 206–10.

tion at its later market-oriented stages, and Christaller's hierarchies most appropriate in analysis of retail and service business in the tertiary sector.[2]

The Market Area for a Good

Assume that identical consumers, distributed at uniform densities over an unbounded plain, can move freely in any direction they choose over this plain.[3] A retailer wants to sell good x; he offers it to consumers at a given price p. However, it costs consumers mt to visit his store to purchase the good (m is the number of miles they live from the store, t is the transport cost per mile [Fig. 3.1]), so the actual price paid by any consumer is $p + mt$. Every consumer has a demand curve for good x such that as price increases, he consumes less of it (Fig. 3.2). This demand curve is the same for each consumer. At price p, q_1 will be consumed, and at price $p + mt$ (the price the consumer pays at distance m), the quantity consumed will be q_2. Thus, a consumer living next to the retailer's store will consume q_1, but because the consumer m miles from the store must pay mt in travel expense, the amount he consumes will be only q_2. Amounts consumed, then, are a function of price to the consumer at his place of residence.

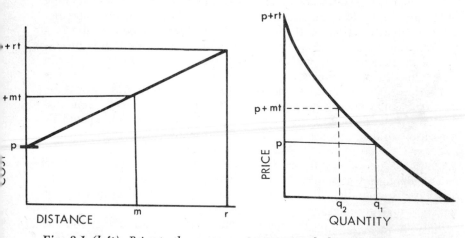

Fig. 3.1 (left). Price to the consumer increases with distance. Fig. 3.2 (right). Quantity consumed declines as price increases.

Since travel is equal in all directions, it is possible to draw a *demand cone* around the store, according to which quantity consumed drops off with distance because of price increases to the consumer due to increased

[2] This is essentially Edwin von Böventer's conclusion in "Towards a Unified Theory of Spatial Economic Structure," *Papers of the Regional Science Association*, Vol. 10 (1962), 163–87.

[3] This *ceteris paribus* assumption is important, for if it can be shown that most of the regularities we have observed can emerge on such a plain, the possibility of causation by spatial differences in raw materials, or unevenness in the distribution of population is eliminated. Theoreticians call the plain we have defined a "transport surface."

Fig. 3.3. *The spatial demand cone.*

transport costs (Fig. 3.3). At distance r, price is $p + rt$ (Fig. 3.1) and quantity consumed is zero (Fig. 3.2). This is the maximum possible economic reach of the store. The "ideal" trade area of the store is a perfect circle with radius r.

Total quantity of good x consumed by customers within this maximum reach r may be obtained by calculating the area, D, beneath the demand cone. Since quantity demanded, q, varies in response to level of retail price plus transport cost, $p + mt$, D is found by integrating the function $q = f(p + mt)$ out to the maximum radius r, and multiplying by population density S.

$$D_i = S \int_0^{2\pi} \left[\int_0^{m=r} f(p_i + mt)\,m\,dm \right] d\theta$$

If this calculation is repeated for a variety of different store selling prices, p_i, cones of varying heights and maximum radii will result, and different levels of total demand D_i may be calculated. If these values of p_i and D_i are plotted in a graph and a line is fitted to the results, an aggregate demand curve D for the market area can be drawn, as in Figure 3.4. At price p_1 the total demand beneath the cone will be D_1, but if this retail store price drops to p_2, aggregate demand increases to D_2, because the demand cone is much larger. If the retailer's long-run average cost curve C is now added to Figure 3.4, the conclusion is that the maximum possible size of store is one providing for an aggregate demand for good x of exactly D_m, offered to consumers at a store price of p_m. Only if the demand curve D and the cost curve C intersect will it be possible to operate a retail store offering good x. Only where D and C cross is some optimum achieved, for elsewhere, at any given price, there would be unmet demands or excess supplies.[4] The resulting price at the retail store, p_m, will yield a particular set of prices $p_m + mt$ to consumers at their place of residence. Since each consumer has the same individual demand curve (Fig. 3.2), the demand cone that can be drawn will have height q_m determined by store price p_m, and a maximum radius r where $p_m + rt$ leads to zero demand.

[4] The long-run average cost curve is used on the grounds that we are looking for the theoretical optimum. Thus, the businessman is allowed to construct exactly that size of store that is optimum. Since, in the solution, changes in market conditions are not considered, the short-run average cost curve (production function) charting the individual businessman's cost variations as his given plant is used for different levels of output is not relevant. The long-run average cost curve (Lösch calls it a planning curve) is an envelope tangent to the short-run average cost curves at the lowest point possible at each level of output.

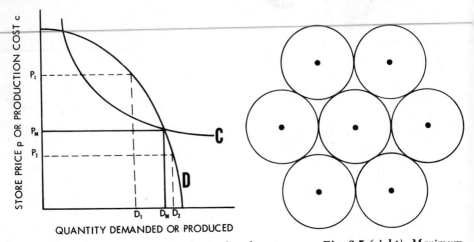

Fig. 3.4 (left). Aggregate demand and cost curves. Fig. 3.5 (right). Maximum packing of tangent circles.

The Network of Trade Areas for a Single Good

If a maximum number of such circular trade areas of maximum radius r is packed into the plain, what will be their spatial arrangement? The amount of vacant, unserved area will be least and the packing maximized where the stores form a triangular-hexagonal pattern, and each trade area is tangential to six others (Fig. 3.5).[5]

If we add the requirement that all consumers be served (i.e., there be no unserved area *between* market areas), then the circles must overlap, and businessmen will have to compete for consumers within the area of overlap (Fig. 3.6).[6] But if the consumers are rational beings who want to consume as much as they can for their money, they will visit the closest store to save transport costs; the areas of overlap will be bisected, and the trade areas will become hexagons (Fig. 3.7). Even though stores compete for consumers in the areas of overlap, the outcome of this spatial competition is determined entirely by assumptions of consumer rationality—that they know the alternatives and choose the cheapest among them, because the quantity they can consume will then be the greatest.

[5] D. Hilbert and S. Cohn-Vosson, *Geometry and the Imagination* (New York: Chelsea, 1957), p. 35. These authors show that a hexagonal lattice is the one which packs the centers of tangent circles closest, while a square lattice is the loosest. Further (p. 85), lattices of points in cells of bilateral symmetry are the only sets that will fill a two-dimensional space such as our transport surface.

[6] Figure 3.6 is taken from C. J. Galpin, *op. cit.*, who concluded "if all the conditions relating to farm homes and neighboring trade centers were conceived to be equal, then apparently the agricultural community would be in the form of a circle." The black area he identified as that in which farm residents made exclusive use of one center, but in the shaded areas he observed that farmers actually use more than one center because they are indifferent.

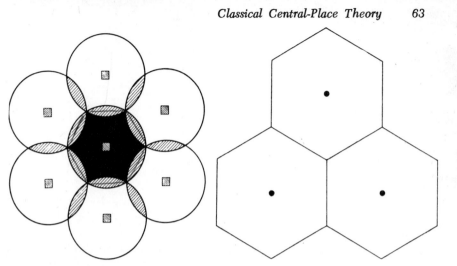

Fig. 3.6 (left). Overlapping circles create areas of competition. Fig. 3.7 (right). Consumer choice leads to hexagonal market areas.

Since the market area then becomes a hexagon rather than a circle, total demand must drop for a given store price p_m because outer positions of the circle have been cut off. The integral derived earlier no longer applies; D must be reduced on the basis of loss of consumers at the edge. A new aggregate demand curve results, as with the dotted line in Figure 3.8.

Another assumption may now be added. If there is complete freedom of entry of stores, the process of spatial competition will be intensified by the packing of more and more businessmen into the plain. Spacing of stores must become closer and closer, there will be increased overlap of circular trade areas, and rational consumer choices minimizing distances traveled will resolve the areas of overlap into smaller hexagonal market areas. For every increase in the number of businessmen,[7] the aggregate demand curve D will drop. The maximum possible packing of businessmen into the plain is achieved where D has dropped to be tangential with the long-run cost curve C, at price p_n and aggregate demand D_n (see Fig. 3.8). This solution is one of imperfect or monopolistic competition: the plain is served by a maximum number of identical, minimum-scale businessmen offering good x at identical prices to hexagonal trade areas of identical minimum size, and no surplus profits are possible.

Christaller's Urban Hierarchies

Assume that a large number of goods and services have to be provided for each of the consumers on the plain. Let the businesses providing these goods be ranked in descending order of the minimum-sized market areas necessary to make each of them just profitable. Use the highest-

[7] And, with our long-run assumption, automatic adjustment of store sizes to an optimum.

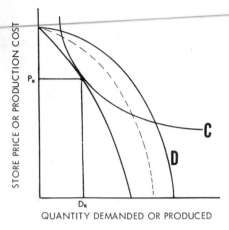

QUANTITY DEMANDED OR PRODUCED   *Fig. 3.8. Long-run equilibrium.*

order good to derive a set of store locations and hexagonal market areas covering the plain, such that the pattern is a long-run optimum (maximum number of stores, minimum size of market areas). Where will stores providing lower-order goods locate, and what will their market areas be like?

Christaller argued that each highest-order store location defines a central place from which all other goods and services will be provided. But the minimum size of market area required for support of successively lower-order goods will be progressively less than the hexagons for the highest-order good. The problem is to find at what point and for what good an enterprising businessman will succeed at a location other than one of the "metropolitan" centers already defined. The answer is found geometrically. Given that existing centers already provide all goods, it will be at a location exactly at the midpoint between three of the original places. The good will be one whose threshold market area around the new location is a hexagon exactly equal to the hexagonal market area for the same good as provided by each of the three existing centers. New centers providing the good may be located at the midpoint of every triangle of three metropolitan centers, and a second network of hexagons can be drawn completely covering the plain. All goods with threshold requirements greater than hexagons of the smaller set and less than or equal to the larger are provided exclusively by the larger centers. All other goods may be provided by both levels of centers.

Repeating the argument a third, fourth, and succeeding times leads to a hierarchy of centers and market areas, and a grouping of goods into orders based upon market area sizes (Fig. 3.9). Each lower-level center is located at the midpoint between three higher-order centers. Market area sizes are minimized for the good which defines each level of the hierarchy. Every higher-order center is surrounded by a ring of six centers of next lower order located at the six points of its hexagon. Thus, for every center of highest order, there are, on the average, three market areas of next lower size (its own, plus one-third of each of the six sur-

Fig. 3.9. A hierarchy according to
Christaller's marketing principle.

rounding, each of which is shared with two other centers), and two places of next lower-order size (each of the ring of six surrounding centers lies on the hexagon of three centers of higher order). The progression of centers by size class runs 1, 2, 6, 18, 54, ..., and the progression of market areas of each level is 1, 3, 9, 27, 81, ...

Because of the competitive nature of the solution, with the market areas of different goods and services drawn together only by the assumption that the largest places will provide all of them, Christaller said the system was organized by a *marketing principle*. The progressive increase of numbers of market areas at successively lower levels of the hierarchy by a rule of threes led Lösch to call it a $K = 3$ network. This K, for market areas, equals the bifurcation ratio k for centers plus one. Complementing the resulting central-place hierarchy is a corresponding hierarchy of transport routes. Each metropolis possesses six major radiating routes linking it to regional cities, plus six secondary routes (Fig. 3.10).

Christaller also proposed two alternative hierarchies, based upon what he termed the *transport principle* and the *administrative principle*.

According to the transport principle, once the triangular-hexagonal distribution of the metropolitan centers and their market areas is derived, the next lower order of centers must locate at the midpoints of the transport routes running directly between these metropolitan centers. Thus, instead of a new center lying midway between three of the metropolises, new centers locate between each pair of them. Although the resulting pattern of hexagonal market areas differs somewhat from that of the marketing principle, a hierarchy is produced maximizing the number of centers located on major transport routes. Because centers locate at midpoints, they bisect the sides of the hexagons rather than locating at their apexes. Since each lower-order place lies on the hexagons of only two higher-order places, the progression of numbers of centers by level is 1, 3, 12, 48, 172, ..., and of market areas is 1, 4, 16, 64, 236, ..., or increasing by a rule of fours ($K = 4$). The spatial pattern and transport routes are indicated in Figure 3.11.

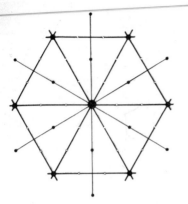

Fig. 3.10. Transportation routes in the K = 3 hierarchy.

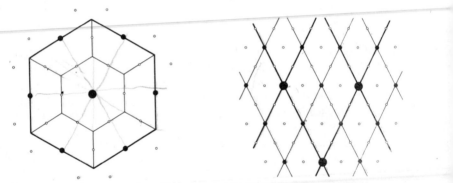

Fig. 3.11. Market areas, center locations, and transport routes in the K = 4 hierarchy.

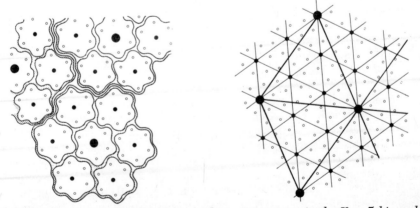

Fig. 3.12. Arrangement, nesting, and transport routes in the K = 7 hierarchy.

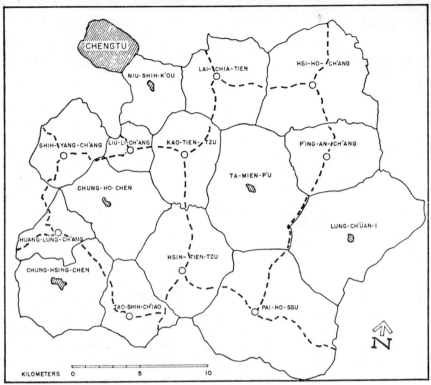

Fig. 3.13. A portion of Szechwan near Chengtu.

Fig. 3.14. First abstraction of Figure 3.13.

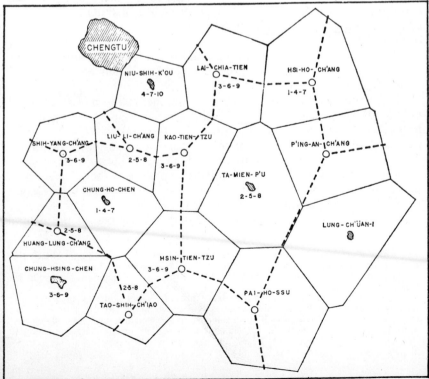

The administrative principle required that each higher-order center completely control a surrounding ring of six lower-order places to allow a proper areal division of powers, so that $K = 7$ (see Fig. 3.12).

Lest these principles seem too abstract or theoretical, Figures 3.13 to 3.18 show the $K = 3$ and $K = 4$ hierarchies as they exist in a part of rural China.[8] In Figure 3.13, a portion of Szechwan southeast of Chengtu is depicted, showing two levels of centers, "standard" markets such as Pai-ho-ssu and larger "intermediate" markets such as Chung-ho-chen, with their market areas. A first abstraction is achieved in Figure 3.14 by straightening out market area boundaries. Reducing Figure 3.14 to diagrammatic form yields the perfect $K = 3$ network of Figure 3.15. A similar sequence (Figs. 3.16 to 3.18) in an area of Szechwan lying 35 to 90 kilometers northeast of Chengtu yields Figure 3.18, a perfect $K = 4$ network except for one empty cell in the mountains.

Discussion of periodic markets in Chapters 5 and 6 will make extensive use of these illustrations. Their introduction in the present context leads to the important conclusion that a theory based upon very simple assumptions predicts market center patterns observable in reality, with only minor local variability. Classical central-place theory therefore begins to provide a scientific basis for understanding the geography of retail and service business, although many of the systematic variations described in Part 1 remain unaccounted for in the Christaller statement.

The Löschian Economic Landscape

Agreeing with Christaller on the hexagonal geometry of a long-run equilibrium, Lösch developed a contrasting picture of systems of location. Christaller built his hierarchies from the highest-order good down, laying out his metropolitan centers first; Lösch built his from the lowest-order good upwards.[9] Christaller required that all lower-level center locations take into account locations of larger centers; Lösch derived a variety of optima and tried to assemble these into an over-all pattern.

Lösch begins by assuming a nucleated settlement pattern of agricultural villages distributed in a triangular fashion, rather than a continuous distribution of population over the plain. He then takes the lowest-order good and derives an optimal triangular-hexagonal arrangement of centers and market areas, by the process of obtaining a network for a good already described. In Figure 3.19 this basic pattern is shown as a set of hexagons, each of which includes 18 outlying villages (black dots) plus the central village in which the business is located.

If all higher-order goods have to find their locations in the central

---

[8] Reproduced with permission of the author from G. W. Skinner, "Marketing and Social Structure in Rural China," *Journal of Asian Studies*, Vol. 34 (November 1964). For a similar abstraction in the case of France, see Lalanne's "Essay on the Theory of Railway Systems."

[9] Several authors have suggested that Christaller's procedure is most properly applied to understanding systems of cities laid down in previously sparsely settled areas, whereas Lösch's approach, beginning from the smallest and least specialized centers, is best considered in the context of densely settled areas undergoing economic change.

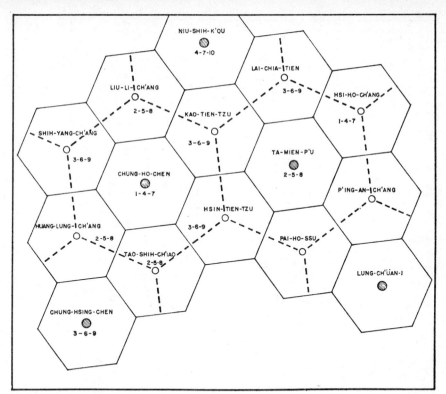

Fig. 3.15. The K = 3 network.

Fig. 3.16. A second portion of Szechwan northeast of Chengtu.

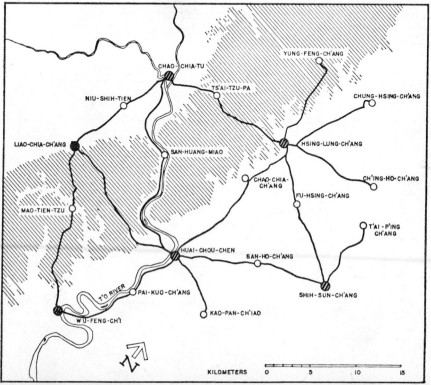

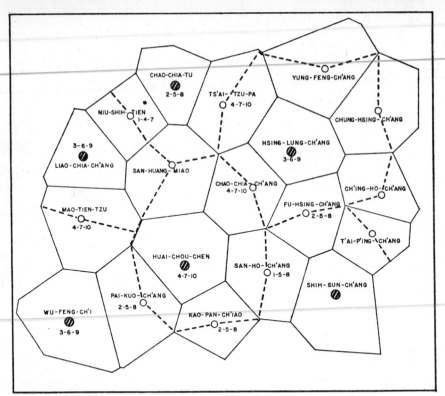

Fig. 3.17. *First abstraction of Figure 3.16.*

Fig. 3.18. *The K = 4 network.*

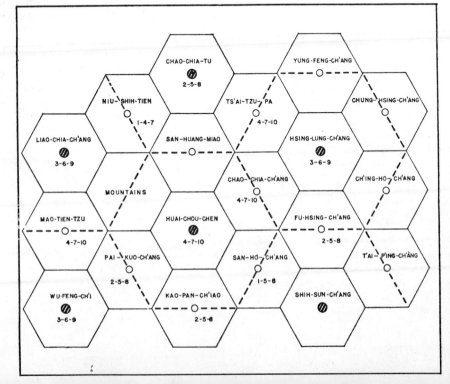

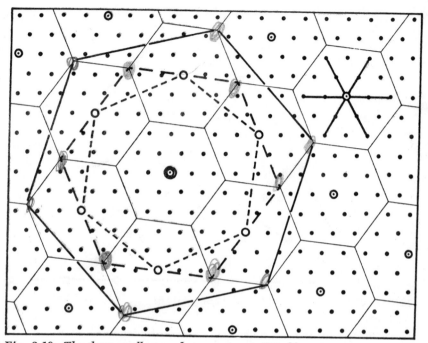

Fig. 3.19. The three smallest market area sizes in Lösch's system.

villages, what will be their location pattern? Lösch argues that all market area requirements ranging from one to three times the basic hexagonal area will locate in a $K = 3$ network. Those with from three to four times the basic hexagon as their condition of entry will locate in a $K = 4$ pattern. Those with thresholds from four to seven times the basic hexagon will locate in a $K = 7$ fashion. The three basic market area sizes are shown in Figure 3.19; compare with Figures 3.9 to 3.12. The next possible market area sizes, in units of the basic hexagon, are up to 9, to 12, 13, 16, 19, 21, 25, ...[10]

Assume in Figure 3.19 that the large dot is the metropolis, and the successive networks of hexagons of increasing size are laid out around it, beginning as shown. Because there is a multiplicity of networks, the functions performed in the villages will differ, but what will be the location pattern? Lösch sets a further requirement: let the different nets be rotated around the metropolis until there is a maximum coincidence or agglomeration of activities in the centers. Figure 3.20 shows the resulting location and functions of villages obtained by Lösch for one 60° sector radiating from the metropolis C, which produces all goods (in ascending order 1, 2, 3, ..., 15 with market areas 1, 3, 4, 7, 9, 12, 13, 16, 19, 21, 25, ... times the basic hexagon). Every village, by definition, produces good 1, but there is considerable specialization in function beyond this

[10] Lösch, *The Economics of Location*, p. 119.

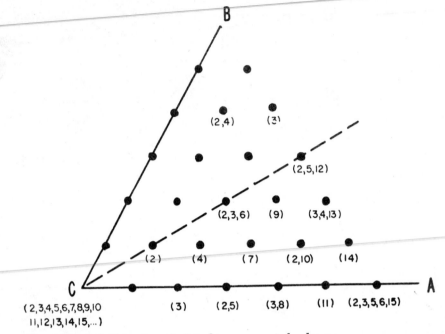

Fig. 3.20. One 60° sector of a Löschian economic landscape.

point. Reading from C to A, the specialties are: none; 3; 2 and 5; 3 and 8; 11; . . . .

The solution is symmetrical in each of six 60° sectors radiating from the metropolis. Each sector also can be divided into two parts, one with intense specialization and one of sparse activity. The result is an *economic landscape* centered on a metropolis and comprising six sectors with many production sites and six with few (Fig. 3.21).

Christaller and Lösch Compared

Both Christaller and Lösch agree that the triangular arrangement of production sites or retail stores, and hexagonal market areas, represents an optimum for a single good, under the assumption of uniform densities on an unbounded plain, with equal access in all directions. Lösch provides explicit proof of this. In the solution, the location of individual firms is as advantageous as possible, every consumer receives service, abnormal profits disappear, market areas are as small as possible, and the boundaries of market areas are points of consumer indifference.

Interlocking networks of markets for different goods are produced in two completely different ways, however. Christaller starts with the highest-threshold good—the "most national" commodity that locates the metropolitan centers—and Lösch starts with the "most local" good. Christaller then produces central-place hierarchies in which there are levels of

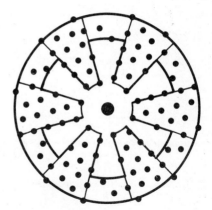

Fig. 3.21. A complete set of Löschian sectors.

centers and groups of goods, in the manner of Table 1.1. Lösch, on the other hand, creates a more diversified economic landscape in which centers specialize. Christaller's formulation appears most relevant for understanding the geography of retail and service business, whereas that of Lösch provides a framework for analyzing the spatial distribution of market-oriented manufacturing.[11] Christaller's agglomerative requirement, for example, is compatible with the idea of travel-cost minimization by rational consumers on multi-purpose trips, a condition not satisfied by Lösch, and the process whereby Christaller locates smaller centers relative to higher-order centers is not unlike the development process observed in Iowa.

[11] E. von Böventer, "Towards a Unified Theory of Spatial Economic Structure," p. 173. However, Tinbergen develops a model of market-oriented location on an isotropic plain, minimizing total costs of production and transportation, and concludes with systems of centers like those of Christaller. Jan Tinbergen, "The Spatial Dispersion of Production: A Hypothesis," *Schweizerische Zeitschrift für Volkswirtschaft und Statistik*, Vol. 97 (1961), 412–19; also his paper "Sur un modèle de la dispersion géographique de l'activité économique," *Revue d'Économie Politique*, Vol. 74 (1964), 30–44.

CHAPTER FOUR

Modern theoretical departures

Modern theorizing has been of several kinds. Attempts to summarize classical theory in mathematical form have led to links with general systems theory. By relaxing assumptions, the applicability of that theory to a wider range of empirical fact has been demonstrated. Most important, Lösch's proof concerning the network of market areas has been extended.

Mathematical Models of the Hierarchy

A first attempt to provide a mathematical model of the hierarchy was by Martin Beckmann,[1] who took the simplest possible case, starting in the manner of Lösch with assumptions of a uniform plain and a network of market areas for a set of lowest-level centers providing the lowest-order good. He then hypothesized that the relationship of population of a center (P_c) and the total population (P_t) served by that center, comprising the trade area population (P_r) plus the center's population (P_c), was

$$P_c = B(P_c + P_r)$$

which can be written

$$P_c = \left(\frac{B}{1-B}\right) P_r$$

and $B/(1-B)$ is the urban multiplier.

His next step, departing from Lösch, assumed a Christaller-type urban

---

[1] "City Hierarchies and the Distribution of City Size," *Economic Development and Cultural Change*, Vol. 6 (April 1958), 243–48. For a comparison of Beckmann's model and Christaller's empirical results for Germany see Marie-Andrée Prost, *La Hiérarchie des Villes* (Paris: Gauthier-Villars, 1965), pp. 70–74.

hierarchy of constant bifurcation ratio k, although, in contrast to Christaller, built from the lowest level upwards. For this hierarchy he wrote

$$P_{tw} = P_{cw} + kP_{t(w-1)}$$

This equation states that the total population served by a center of level w, where w increases from a lowest level of $w = 1$, equals its own population plus the total population served by the k centers of the next lower level that it dominates. In Christaller's $K = 3$ case, this would mean that the total population served by a center of the second level in the hierarchy equals its own population and the population it serves at the first level, plus the total population served by the two centers of lowest level that nest into its trade area. Stated more generally, where P_{r1} is the total population in one of the basic lowest-level trade areas

$$P_{tw} = \frac{k^{w-1} P_{r1}}{(1-B)^w}$$

and

$$P_{cw} = \frac{Bk^{w-1} P_{r1}}{(1-B)^w}$$

Both city size and population served increase exponentially as level in the hierarchy increases, a fact matching exactly the empirical observation (Chapter 2) that the number of business types in a town progresses with level of center in the form $T_{cw} = dk^{w-1}$, d being a factor varying with population densities. All characteristics of central places thus far studied also vary exponentially with level of center in the hierarchy: total population served, population of center, number of establishments, traffic generated, number of different types of business provided, and so on. Many graphs indicating this have already been presented.[2]

This kind of variation implies that the percentage change in any one of these variables is constant with movement from one step of the hierarchy to another. That is, if E indicates establishments in a center and C is a constant

$$\frac{dE}{Edw} = C$$

and

$$w = C^{-1} \log E$$

A similar expression could be presented for each of the other characteristics. Where functions of this form are found, hierarchical organization

---

[2] The semi-logarithmic form of Figures 2.4, 2.11, 2.12, and 2.14 might imply the contrary for business types. The apparent linearity (for example, in Fig. 2.14, $\log P_c = 2.095 + 0.02T$, with a correlation of 0.95) is undoubtedly due to the fact that we have only a few levels of center, and that the classification of business types used was insensitive to increased specialization of functions with increasing level in the hierarchy. The descriptive model I presented in "Aggregate Relations and Elemental Components of Central Place Systems," *Journal of Regional Science*, Vol. 4, No. 1 (1962), 35–68, is limited in this respect, although the implications drawn are not affected.

must be present and the hierarchy *must* have a regular bifurcation ratio. Only then will the necessary constant proportional relationships between higher and lower levels of the hierarchy hold. The degree to which such functions may be observed is the degree to which there is hierarchical organization.[3]

Passage into General Systems Theory

A strict hierarchy would demand the centers of any level of the hierarchy to have exactly identical populations. Beckmann showed that if populations of centers were allowed to vary somewhat around the expected value for their level, as if a random disturbance factor were operating, and if centers were then ranked in decreasing order of size, $P_1, P_2, P_3 \ldots, P_r, \ldots, P_n$, subscript indicating rank, the products of size and rank would approximate a constant. That is, $P_1 \times 1 = P_2 \times 2 = P_3 \times 3 = \ldots = P_r \times r = $ constant.

This relationship, observed many times all over the world, was popularized by G. K. Zipf [4] as the *rank-size rule*, which he expressed in the form $P_r = P_1/r^q$, where q is an exponent which generally approximates unity. Figure 4.1, illustrates the regularity for the United States from 1790 through 1950. Much analysis in the quarter-century since Zipf did his work leads to the conclusion that the regularity will result wherever the rate of relative population growth of centers at any level of the hierarchy is, on the average, a constant fraction of the rate of relative population growth of the entire hierarchy of centers.[5] The rank-size rule is the equilibrium or steady-state of such a growth process.

This observation ties central-place theory to *general systems theory*. General systems theory provides exactly what it suggests: a general theory of systems. *A system is a set of objects* (for example, central places), *attributes of the objects* (population, establishments, business types, traffic generated), *interrelations among the objects* (midpoint locations

---

[3] I pointed this out initially in "Retail Location and Consumer Behavior," *Papers and Proceedings of the Regional Science Association,* Vol. 9 (1962), 65–106. The stimulus came from *information theory,* in which the information in a number of states is $H = C \log S$. If the states were simply noise, they would be randomly distributed and no information would exist at all, only a condition of entropy. Organization in the states provides information, however, or what is termed "macroscopic negative entropy (negentropy)." In the paper I used business types as a measure of information, instead of level of center w. This stemmed from the limited number of levels of centers in the case study, and needs correction.

[4] G. K. Zipf, *National Unity and Disunity* (Bloomington: Principia Press, 1941). Since many characteristics of centers are highly correlated, the relationship should apply not only to population, but to sales, establishments, and other factors.

[5] This is the biologists' *law of allometric growth.* Where y is the organ and x is the organism, $(dy/dt)(1/y) = b(dx/dt)(1/x)$ so that $\int(dy/y) = b\int(dx/x)$ and $\log y = \log a + b \log x$. Various other ways of generating rank-size distributions have been proposed, using probability theory; these are reviewed in my paper "Cities as Systems within Systems of Cities," *Papers of the Regional Science Association,* Vol. 13 (1964), 147–64.

SIZE

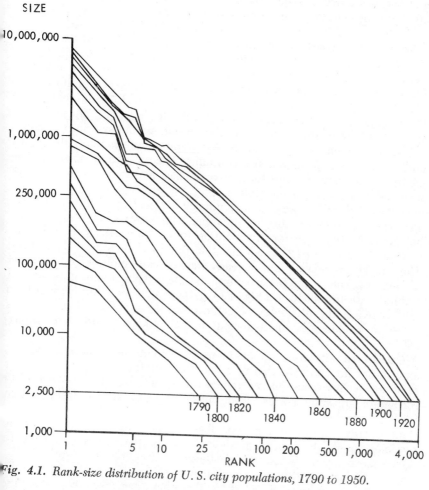

Fig. 4.1. Rank-size distribution of U. S. city populations, 1790 to 1950.

or lower-level centers, uniform spacing at any given level) *and among he attributes* (the graphs of log-log relationships), *and interdependencies f objects and attributes* (the central-place hierarchy). Two kinds of ystems are often identified by the systems theorists. *Closed systems* are ntirely self-contained; *open systems* exchange energy (materials, mes-ages, and ideas) with a surrounding environment.

Closed systems have a given energy supply available to do work. As ork is performed the energy is dissipated and will eventually become ndomly distributed throughout the system. Using the terminology of e second law of thermodynamics, the system will then have reached a ndition of maximum entropy.[6] If a central-place system were closed

---

[6] Ludwig von Bertalanffy, "General System Theory," *General Systems*, Vol. 1 956), 1–10.

and had run down to a state of maximum entropy, population and other attributes of centers would be completely unrelated to level of centers in the hierarchy. In fact, any trace of a hierarchy would vanish.

With relative constancy in energy inputs and approximate balance of inputs and outputs, open systems settle into an organized equilibrium between the tendency to move toward maximum entropy and the need for organization to perform· work. Such an organized equilibrium is called a *steady-state*. A central-place system is open. Energy inputs come from the demands of consumers, who constitute the "environment" of the system. Demands are balanced by the outputs of the system, the goods and services supplied to consumers. Assuming a uniform plain, the inputs and outputs will have relative constancy over a period of time. The central-place hierarchy is a form of organization that performs the work involved as efficiently as possible.

However, there is always some tendency for local variability, so perfect conformity to the steps of the hierarchy is not expected. A steady-state balances (1) the need for organization into a hierarchy to perform the work efficiently, and (2) randomization due to chance local differences. The rank-size regularity is this steady-state. It can be observed at a point in time. It develops and persists through time if the system is growing and maintains a constant form (Fig. 4.1). Exponential relationships will then exist between the attributes of centers and levels of the hierarchy, as noted in Beckmann's mathematical model, and demonstrated empirically.[7]

Any decrease in energy inputs increases the entropy in an open system, and causes adjustments changing the form of the steady-state. By the same token, increasing energy inputs cause form adjustments leading to further organization (or negative entropy). Open systems also contain feedback mechanisms that affect growth even under conditions of constant energy inputs. Positive feedback would tend to decrease the randomizing effects of local variability, and negative feedback to increase them, thus respectively increasing either organization or entropy.[8]

One conclusion of the general systems theorists is worthy of note: the steady-state in an open system is one that obeys principles of *equifinality* Whatever the initial sizes of the central places, the same steady-state wil. be achieved provided the energy flows are the same. The steady-state results solely from energy flows, independent of the initial size conditions Thus, a rank-size relationship will result solely from the balance of loca variability and the organizational needs for a hierarchy under a given

---

[7] Zipf's thesis, in *National Unity and Disunity*, was that the rule can be foun when separate closed local socio-economic systems have been linked into large national systems, and in *Human Behavior and the Principle of Least Effort* (Cam bridge: Addison-Wesley, 1949) he went on to argue that the move from loc: variability to a national system was to minimize effort. Thus, he had in his work th germ of the systems theory, organization, and steady-state concepts.

[8] M. Maruyama, in "The Second Cybernetics: Deviation Amplifying Mutu: Causal Processes," *The American Scientist*, Vol. 51 (1963), 164–79, discusses pos tive feedback mechanisms involving circular and cumulative causation. In centra place systems, they are represented by the tendency of consumers to prefer larg centers and bypass the smaller, which permits the larger to grow and constra the smaller.

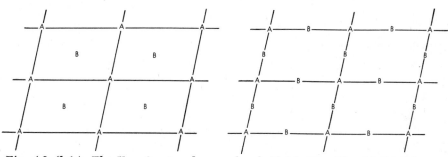

Fig. 4.2 (left). *The K = 2 network on a rhomboidal lattice.* **Fig. 4.3 (right).** *The K = 3 network.*

set of demand and supply conditions. This is also a characteristic of the competitive model used to derive a central-place system.

Alternative Geometries [9]

Christaller's model, which assumed the uniform plain was a transport surface, displayed a triangular-hexagonal distribution of highest level centers, and subsequent $K = 3$, 4, or 7 hierarchies depending upon whether the special assumptions related to minimization of consumer travel, location of lower-level centers on the transport routes joining the highest-level centers, or administrative convenience.

At least one alternative geometry may be proposed. If the highest-order centers are arranged on a rectangular or rhomboidal lattice, consistent application of Christaller's argument would still lead to locations of lower-level centers at midpoints. If the midpoint location is selected in the manner of his marketing principle, Figure 4.2 results. The A's are centers of highest order, located on the rhomboidal lattice; the B's are centers of next order. Each A center is surrounded by a ring of four B centers, but each of the B centers is simultaneously on the rings of four A centers. Thus $k = 1$, for there are just as many B-level centers as there are those of A-level, and $K = 2$.

By following Christaller's transport principle, Figure 4.3 results. The B centers are required to locate at the midpoints of transport routes joining the A centers. Since each B center lies on the market area boundary between two A centers, there are twice as many B centers as A centers, and $k = 2$ with $K = 3$. By the same token, k should equal 4 and $K = 5$ for the rectangular-rhomboidal administrative principle, with two alternative spatial patterns, as indicated in Figure 4.4.

These examples indicate that the outcome of a central-place model is dependent upon initial assumptions about the existing spatial system. In the United States the rhomboidal or rectangular lattice seems most relevant, but in China a triangular-hexagonal pattern may be more appropriate (Figs. 3.13 to 3.18). The value of Beckmann's model is that it

[9] Michael F. Dacey, in "The Geometry of Central Place Theory," *Geografiska Annaler*, Vol. 47B (1965), 111–24, provides a suitable mathematical system for examining traditional and alternative geometries.

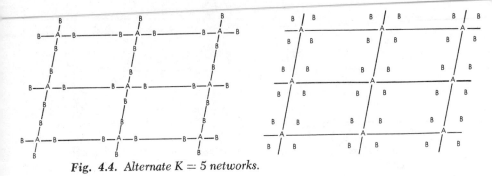

Fig. 4.4. *Alternate K = 5 networks.*

applies with any basic geometry. Taking, for example, the expression $T_{cw} = dk^{w-1}$, we obtain

$$\log_k T_{cw} = \log_k d + (w - 1)$$

The bifurcation ratio k provides the base for the logarithms, and the w's are integers in base k logarithms. Given Christaller's models, the base of the logarithms could be 2, 3, or 6, and in Iowa, 1, 2, or 4 are possible (in the study area it was 2).

Generalization of Lösch's Market Area Equilibrium

In Chapter 3 the individual demand curve was presented as $f(p_i + mt)$, but the shape of that function was not specified. The aggregate demand function was left as

$$D_i = S \int_0^{2\pi} \left[\int_0^{m=r} f(p_i + mt)\,m\,dm \right] d\theta$$

and the shape of the firm's cost curve was not defined.

Let both the cost and the individual demand functions be linear:

$$C = F + cu$$

where F is fixed costs, u is number of units sold, and c is variable cost per unit, and

$$q_i = g - h(p_i + mt)$$

where q_i is quantity consumed by the family, p_i is at-store price, t is transport costs per mile, and m is number of miles of residence from the store.

Therefore, for a circular market area,

$$D_i = S \int_0^{2\pi} \left\{ \int_0^{m=r} [g - h(p_i + mt)]\,m\,dm \right\} d\theta$$

where S is population densities and r is maximum radius consumers wil travel. Similarly, for market areas of other figures displaying bilateral symmetry,

$$D_i = 2nS \int_0^{\pi/n} \left\{ \int_0^{m/\cos\theta} [g - h(p_i + mt)]m\,dm \right\} d\theta$$

where n is number of sides of the figure and m is distance from center of figure to midpoint of its sides.

Since a firm's total profit R is

$$R = p_i \, D_i - (F + cD_i)$$
$$= D_i \, (p_i - c) - F$$

the results of evaluating the integrals for a triangle ($\triangle$), square ($\square$), hexagon ($\bigcirc$), and circle ($\bigcirc$) are

$$R_\triangle = 6Sr^2 \left(\frac{\sqrt{3}}{2} g - \frac{\sqrt{3}}{2} hp_i - .7069\, htr \right) (p_i - c) - F$$

$$R_\square = 8Sr^2 \left(\frac{g}{2} - \frac{hp_i}{2} - .3848\, htr \right) (p_i - c) - F$$

$$R_\bigcirc = 12Sr^2 \left(\frac{g}{2\sqrt{3}} - \frac{hp_i}{2\sqrt{3}} - .2027\, htr \right) (p_i - c) - F$$

$$R_\bigcirc = 2\pi Sr^2 \left(\frac{g}{2} - \frac{hp_i}{2} - \frac{htr}{3} \right) (p_i - c) - F$$

Given population densities S, and the demand curve for individuals $g - h (p_i + mt)$, plus cost function of the business $F + cu$, the above equations indicate that the firm's profits will depend upon price charged (p_i) and the maximum distance consumers will travel (r). In fact, solving the relevant differential equations with respect to p_i and m yields the information contained in Table 4.1.[10] For the profit maximizing distance m, the price charged will be the same whatever the market area form:

$$p_i = \frac{g}{2h} + \frac{c}{2} - 0.25 \left(\frac{g - hc}{ht} \right)$$

However, maximum profits will not be the same; they are least for the triangle and most for the circle, further proof of the contention that firms prefer circular market areas.

Some other conclusions are worthy of note. For a given transport rate per mile t, to increase the maximum distance r consumers are willing to travel, the firm must decrease price p. As m increases, mt increases faster than p decreases, so delivered price at the perimeter increases and demand per family falls. This is consistent with the observation that real

[10] These solutions were provided by Edwin S. Mills and Michael R. Lav in "A Model of Market Areas with Free Entry," *Journal of Political Economy,* Vol. 72 (June 1964), 278–90. See also R. E. Kuenne, *The Theory of General Economic Equilibrium* (Princeton: Princeton Univ., 1963), pp. 451–52.

Table 4.1. Solutions to Market Area Equations

Shape of Area

	Triangle	Square	Hexagon	Circle
Profit maximizing m	$.5434 \left(\dfrac{g - hc}{ht} \right)$	$.6534 \left(\dfrac{g - hc}{ht} \right)$	$.7121 \left(\dfrac{g - hc}{ht} \right)$	$.7501 \left(\dfrac{g - hc}{ht} \right)$
Maximum profit	$.0959 \left[\dfrac{(g - hc)^4}{g^3 t^2} \right] S - F$	$.1067 \left[\dfrac{(g - hc)^4}{g^3 t^2} \right] S - F$	$.1098 \left[\dfrac{(g - hc)^4}{g^3 t^2} \right] S - F$	$.1104 \left[\dfrac{(g - hc)^4}{g^3 t^2} \right] S - F$
Profit minimizing m	$1.0863 \left(\dfrac{g - hc}{ht} \right)$	$1.3070 \left(\dfrac{g - hc}{ht} \right)$	$1.4242 \left(\dfrac{g - hc}{ht} \right)$	$1.5000 \left(\dfrac{g - hc}{ht} \right)$
Minimum profit	$-F$	$-F$	$-F$	$-F$

incomes and levels of living are lowest on the interurban periphery (see Chapter 8). As m goes to zero, sales go to zero and the firm loses fixed cost F.

What will be the pattern of market areas for a set of firms on a uniform plain, given free entry? The basic idea of *free entry in spatial competition* is that firms will continue to enter into activity on the plain so long as there is some pattern of market areas that will permit more firms per square mile, with all firms making at least zero profits.[11] Lösch contended that the hexagonal pattern of market areas provided maximum packing because, for a given m, hexagons permit more firms in an area than squares, and these in turn more than triangles, whereas tangent circles leave unserved area; Lösch argued that all consumers must be served.

If the second row of Table 4.1 is examined, it will be seen that each of the equations has the form

$$\left\{ z \left[\frac{(g - hc)^4}{g^3 t^2} \right] S - F \right\},$$

and z is .0959 (triangle), .1067 (square), .1098 (hexagon), and .1104 (circle). For zero profits, the left side of the equation must equal the right side, fixed costs F. It is possible to find a level of fixed costs F such that *no* firms with hexagonal market areas can break even. Lösch's contention that the set of market areas must completely fill the plain, and that there be no unserved consumers, is thus invalid. If F is less than $\{.1098[(g - hc)^4/g^3 t^2]S\}$, Lösch's contention is correct. If it is not, then some unserved area will remain.

The solution for unserved area need not be a set of tangent circles, as in Figure 3.5. Given a set of tangent circles, it is possible to circumscribe about the circles dodecagons (12-sided regular polygons) such that pairs of parallel sides of adjoining dodecagons are tangent at the point of tangency of the circles. The circles and dodecagons have the same m, and there are just as many centers and market areas, but the dodecagons serve more customers. The argument can be generalized for any regular n-sided polygons where n is a multiple of six. For such figures, the maximum profits will be between the $\{.1098[(g - hc)^4/g^3 t^2]S - F\}$ of the hexagon and the $\{.1104[(g - hc)^4/g^3 t^2]S - F\}$ of the circle. It is therefore possible to select a level of fixed costs F such that the zero-profit m for an n-sided polygon is less than the zero-profit m for tangent circles, while F is too great for hexagonal market areas to break even. The n-sided polygons then give the equilibrium market area pattern, which lies between the space-filling hexagons and the tangent circles, with some unserved customers.[12]

An Alternative Demand Curve

Many alternatives to the simple linear demand function of the previous section are possible; one of the more important is that of Baumol

---

[11] Mills and Lav, *ibid.*
[12] *Ibid.*

and Ide,[13] which sets the solution for a single good within the context of a set of goods. Baumol and Ide define the following:

$p(T)$ = The probability that a consumer will find the goods he needs to make his trip a success in the center that offers T goods.

mt = The costs of traveling m miles to the center at t per mile.

$c_n \sqrt{T}$ = The difficulty of shopping, emerging out of size and congestion, defined as costs proportional to the square root of the size of center T.

c_i = The opportunity costs of alternative activities foregone, including other shopping opportunities.

The consumer, it is argued, will not shop at a store unless $f(t,m) = e[p(T)] - l(mt + c_n \sqrt{T} + c_i)$ is positive. Constants e and l are, respectively, the subjective weighting functions assigned by the consumer to his expectation of success (e will also be affected by price levels, since the probability of success is the probability of achieving wants at a price), and his feelings concerning costs involved (l). Solving for the maximum distance consumers are willing to travel to shop yields

$$r = \frac{e}{lt} p(T) - \frac{1}{t} (c_n \sqrt{T} + c_i)$$

Increased variety is important to consumers up to a point. The minimum number of items needed to induce a consumer to a center must increase with distance from the center, m, but the optimum variety is independent of distance.

Suppose that the store's sales depend directly upon the number of individuals who can be induced to shop there, and that at any distance m, the function $f(T,m)$ gives the proportion of consumers who will shop there.[14] Then, with a uniform plain of population density S, the aggregate demand will be

$$D_i = S \int_0^{2\pi} \left\{ \int_0^r \left[(ep(T) - l(c_n \sqrt{T} + c_i)) - ltm \right] mdm \right\} d\theta$$

$$= 2\pi Sr^2 \left[\frac{ep(T) - l(c_n \sqrt{T} + c_i)}{2} - lt\frac{r}{3} \right]$$

But

$$r = \frac{ep(T) - l(c_n \sqrt{T} + c_i)}{lt}$$

[13] W. J. Baumol and E. A. Ide, "Variety in Retailing," *Management Science* Vol. 3 (October 1956), 93–101.
[14] Or, alternatively, argue that all consumers within r will shop there, but that $f(T,m)$ describes the proportional decline in per capita purchases with distance.

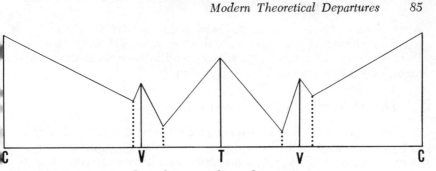

Fig. 4.5. *Cross section through a set of demand cones.*

Therefore, substituting:

$$D_i = \frac{1}{3} \, lt\pi S r^3$$

If it is assumed that population densities are not uniform, but vary from a point of maximum concentration S at the store inversely with distance S/m, then the results become

$$D_i = S \int_0^{2\pi} \left\{ \int_0^r [ep(T) - l(c_n \sqrt{T} + c_i) - ltm]dm \right\} d\theta$$

$$= 2\pi S \left\{ [ep(T) - l(c_n \sqrt{T} + c_i)] \, m - \frac{ltm^2}{2} \right\}_0^r$$

$$= lt\pi S r^2$$

In both cases aggregate demand is a function of maximum distance consumers are willing to travel, r, but on the uniform plain it varies as the cube of distance, whereas if population densities drop inversely with distance from the center, it varies with the square of distance.[15]

This model has certain valuable features. It points out why in Figure 2.3, and through Figures 1.13 to 1.19, larger centers have larger market areas for a given good. Even if prices were the same in all centers, and costs per mile of traveling were identical, larger centers would have larger market areas because of the greater probability that consumers will find all their needs satisfied on a multi-purpose shopping trip.[16]

Prices will generally be lower in the larger center, and transport costs less for any single good because of the multi-purpose nature of the trip. A cross section through a set of demand cones in Iowa must appear as in Figure 4.5, taking all cost elements into account. Demand is greatest

---

[15] The latter case is, from the points of view of both distance and the squared distance character of the aggregate, very close to the arguments of social physicists about the geographic patterns of many phenomena. See J. Q. Stewart, "Potential of Population and its Application to Marketing," in Reavis Cox and Wroe Alderson, *Theory in Marketing* (Homewood, Ill.: Irwin, 1950), pp. 19–40. Also refer back to Chapter 2 on the "law of retail gravitation."

[16] W. L. Garrison, et al., *Studies of Highway Development and Geographic Change* (Seattle: Univ. of Washington, 1959), pp. 197–226.

nearer larger centers because of lower prices, greater variety of goods, and lower transport rate. Therefore, the size of market areas varies with level of center in the hierarchy; villages tend to have asymmetric market areas, deflected away from the largest center.

The Debate on Spatial Competition

Free entry results in long-run equilibrium at the point of tangency between the aggregate demand curve and the long-run average cost curve (Fig. 3.8). Therefore, store price equals average cost. This is a characteristic of conditions of *monopolistic competition*, for in a classical, perfectly competitive solution, store price would have to equal marginal cost.[17]

Actually, competitive *product-differentiation*, which is the basis of monopolistic competition, has a threefold foundation. Firms in competition aspire to maximize profits by seeking a combination of three economic variables: adjustments of location in space, changes in quality of product, and price. Economists increasingly use the term "competition" to refer to *price* competition, relatively neglecting *spatial* competition and competition in *quality*.

The classic economic model of spatial competition is that of Hotelling,[18] who assumed two sellers (for example, ice cream vendors) and buyers uniformly distributed along a line (a beach) and showed that, contrary to expectations, they would cluster at the midpoint of the line rather than at the quartiles, which would be to the advantage of customers. The reason is that the market boundary lies halfway between the two sellers; each completely commands the linear market on the side away from his competition. For any position other than center, then, it will pay one seller to move closer to his competition to increase his market area. The only stable solution is at the center.

However, if there are more than two sellers, they will be spaced evenly along the beach, as Chamberlin argued in his generalization of Hotelling.[19]

Although Lösch dealt with conditions of monopolistic competition, his presentation appears to have been overlooked in the literature on spatial competition, and thus economics *per se* has come to consider the competitive plane only recently, with a general conclusion that the Hotelling type of center-clustering cannot imply a stable locational equilibrium. The preference is for a Löschian solution.[20]

A discussion of particular significance for understanding differences between the competitive solution within cities and in the countryside (hence the choice of a Reilly or Huff model of market areas) has recently

[17] Mills and Lav explore the welfare implications of the result.
[18] H. Hotelling, "Stability in Competition," *Economic Journal*, Vol. 41 (January 1929), 52–53.
[19] Edward H. Chamberlin, *The Theory of Monopolistic Competition*, 8th ed (Cambridge: Harvard Univ., 1962), pp. 260–65.
[20] Mills and Lav, *op. cit.*

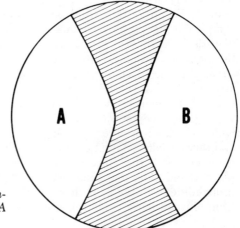

Fig. 4.6. Zones within which consumers are indifferent between A and B.

been provided by Devletoglou.[21] He assumes a uniform plain with equal densities, transport costs that increase linearly with distance, and identical consumers. Initially only two identical firms selling at identical prices are considered (i.e., he is concerned with *duopoly*). Consumers will prefer one or the other firm on the basis of distance, but there is some *minimum sensible* constraint of difference, a minimum difference in travel distance between the stores that the consumers find inconsequential. Given the locations of the two centers, consumers within the zone of overlap defined by this inconsequential distance-difference reveal no spatial preference. Instead, they are subject to a "fashion effect," with a greater likelihood of mass imitation in a larger area. Figure 4.6 shows one such area of overlap for two stores, A and B.

Devletoglou demonstrates that the closer the firms locate together at the center of the plain, the greater the zone of indifference, and the lower the probability that each firm will receive a half-share of the market, or at least greater uncertainty on the part of the businessman. The greater the dispersion, the greater the chance of each firm receiving its half.

On the other hand, there are constraints on how far firms can separate, because of the effects of increased distance on levels of consumer demand. Further, with greater dispersion comes more likelihood of entry by new competition. Thus, "symmetrically mobile duopolists maximize utility in accordance with a subjectively-given pattern of weighing three pertinent variables: the certainty area, average distance travelled by consumers, and the probability of new entry."[22] The result is a Löschian location pattern for the competitors on the plain.

Devletoglou's conception of the effects of minimum sensible distance differences seems of little relevance to central places in rural areas, for

---

[21] Nicos E. Devletoglou, "A Dissenting View of Duopoly and Spatial Competition," *Economica*, Vol. 32 (May 1965), 140–60.
[22] *Ibid.*

the tyranny of distance is so great that areas of indifference are strictly limited. The transition from one market area to another is rapid and complete (Figure 1.13). However, within the city, at high population densities, a variety of centers can achieve at least threshold sales within the *minimum* distance consumers are willing to travel on a shopping trip. Areas of market area overlap are great (Figure 2.25). Preferences are not absolute, but can best be described by probability models for any relatively homogeneous set of centers which describe the likelihood of visiting those centers within some minimum radius of the home, and for which revealed preference seems most affected by the variety of goods and services offered, and only marginally by distance. The fashion effect, combined with the difference in difficulty of shopping in, for example, planned and older unplanned shopping centers, can markedly affect these probabilities, which helps describe the switch in consumers' orientation from older to more modern centers and stores.[23]

---

[23] Bucklin argues that there are several statistically significant factors affecting consumer choice of center: distance, mode of transport, number of shopping stops, income, race, price, variety of products offered, advertising, recommendations by others, and past experience. Louis P. Bucklin, *Consumer Shopping Patterns in an Urban Region* (Berkeley: School of Business, Univ. of California, 1966).

*perspectives
of time and space*

CHAPTER FIVE

Away from the complex:
cross-cultural patterns

Studies undertaken in every country with a complex modern economy show retail and service business hierarchically organized in a central-place system. The general features of this system repeat themselves in each country, regardless of divergent historical traditions.[1] Yet to restrict analysis to such economies ignores the rich variety of marketing and distribution systems in the world as a whole.

Most of the world's people live in peasant societies that are simpler in economic organization than the modern economies that have been the frame of reference up to this point. The way of life in peasant societies combines market activity with subsistence production. Money is used for a wide range of transactions in market-place situations, but there is also production by the household that does not find its way into the market.

Beyond peasant societies, there are still simpler cultures in which exchange takes the form of reciprocal gift-giving or the redistribution of goods, and barter is the rule. Exchange is related to ceremonials associated with the life cycle, social contacts and the establishment of status differentials, ritual, cooperative endeavor, or the cementing of political alliances.

No society can be found in which exchange is absent, although in

---

[1] For example, comparative studies and reviews show that every country in Europe has some or all levels of the same seven-level hierarchy of central places. See M. Goossens, "Hierarchie en Hinterlanden der Centra," *Acta Geographica Lovaniensia*, Vol. 2 (1963); M. Palomäki, "The Functional Centers and Areas of South Bothnia," *Fennia*, Vol. 84 (1964); R. E. Dickinson, *City and Region* (London: Routledge, 1964). Sometimes a country, because of its small size, will not have the upper level. Sometimes the lowest levels are absent for reasons of more advanced transport technology, or unexpectedly still exist, as, for example, in Switzerland, because of the local bases of Swiss democracy, but the same hierarchy otherwise exists. See also H. Gardiner Barnum, *Market Centers and Hinterlands in Baden-Württemberg*, Department of Geography Research Paper No. 103, University of Chicago (1966), in which an analysis exactly parallel to Chapters 1 and 2 of this book is presented.

many, market-place trading is a relatively recent innovation that has spread with the extension of western colonial influence. General factors influential in stimulating market-place development include establishment of law and order, introduction of cash as an exchange medium, expansion of transport facilities, and growth of nonagricultural markets for foodstuffs.

Similarities of Variations Among and Within Complex Economies

Sizes of centers at each level of the hierarchy within a complex economy vary in response to changes in population density. These density shifts still operate when different economies are compared,[2] but additional forces are at work, leading to differences in numbers, kinds, and management of stores. Dominant among additional forces are income differences (demand) and industrial organization (supply). These, in turn, work in similar ways to create regional differences within the economies.

One recent, thorough exercise in comparative marketing analysis [3] points out that the ratio of stores, including service establishments, to population is remarkably similar in Great Britain, the United States, and Canada: one shop for every 74 people in the first two cases, one to 79 people in Canada. However, the relative number of stores in luxury trades is greatest in the United States and lowest in Britain, with exactly the converse true for stores selling necessities, in accordance with income differences between the countries. Moreover, store size and sales productivity of labor are greatest in the United States.

These patterns contrast with consistent trends within rich or poor regions of the three countries. In poor regions, average sales volumes and the ratio of chains to independent stores jump sharply from rural to urban areas, then continue to increase with city size for convenience goods outlets, whereas in rich regions the transition from medium-sized to large cities is marked by relative increase in the number of stores and proportion of independents, and by a decrease in store size. For shopping-goods stores, the chain-independent ratio peaks in medium-sized towns, but store size continues to increase throughout the city size range. In Canada and Britain the peaking of the ratio is found in smaller cities than in the United States.

---

[2] In Europe, sizes of centers at each level vary directly with population densities, and the largest centers of a given level are in the most densely populated areas, roughly in the same range as the American "dispersed city." The dispersed city phenomenon does not exist in that range of densities, however, because of lower mobility levels in Europe. Only within individual metropolitan areas or complex conurbations, at even higher densities, does specialization among centers appear. Similarly, further differences in Finland (Palomäki, *ibid.*, and Helle, footnote 6 below) are related to a combination of very low densities and relatively low incomes.

[3] Margaret Hall, John Knapp, and Christopher Winsten, *Distribution in Great Britain and North America* (Oxford: Oxford Univ., 1961). The study took almost 8 years to complete, much of the time being taken up with reconciliation of differences between censuses—difficulties which in the past have worked against effective comparative studies in marketing.

These findings indicate a consistent tendency within each modern economy for chains to locate only in places that provide some minimum market size, and show the fragmentation of tastes that leads to increased store numbers in the largest cities of the wealthiest regions, where maximum numbers of customers come together in circumstances that also make for the greatest numbers of would-be entrepreneurs.[4] Peaking in smaller centers indicates lower levels of mobility in Britain than in the United States.

Income effects within each of the three countries show the same effects as between them: relative number of convenience-goods stores decreases and that of shopping-goods stores increases with rising income.[5]

British chain stores are more numerous and smaller than their North American counterparts, as are British shopping-goods stores, because of differences in industrial organization and contrasts in the relative costs of labor and capital from one side of the Atlantic to another.

These generalizations can be extended across the whole range of modern economies, yet are insufficient to account for additional kinds of variety that extend across them. For example, where population densities are very low, especially in northern latitudes, the area within the maximum distance consumers are willing to travel to a center is insufficient to support a permanent market. Retailing is therefore conducted by mobile shops,[6] which travel from one population cluster to another to accumulate the necessary volume of demand for survival, selling in sufficient bulk so that the customer can wait until the next visit. In this way, limitations upon the businessman of insufficient aggregate demand and upon the customer of excessive travel distances needed to purchase goods are overcome in a mutually satisfactory way.

The breadth of the generalizations also overlooks the rich local variety that may affect the geography of retailing. An excellent example of variety was recently provided in a study of a part of Ontario in which both Old Order Mennonites and "modern" Canadians live.[7] The Mennonites use modern methods only to manage their farm businesses. In dress, domestic consumption, and travel they retain the habits of two centuries ago: plain homemade clothes are worn, few goods are demanded, and the horse and buggy is the sole means of transportation.

The result is that the set of central places in the area is used in two separate ways; in effect, the two groups have two systems. Where the

---

[4] See also Wilbur Thompson, *A Preface to Urban Economics* (New York: Wiley, 1965); Otis Dudley Duncan, "Urbanization and Retail Specialization," *Social Forces*, Vol. 30 (March 1952), 267–71; Duncan, "Service Industries and the Urban Hierarchy," *Papers and Proceedings of the Regional Science Association*, Vol. 5 (1959), 105–20.

[5] Similar differences in the character of centers have also been noted within large American cities. See my *Commercial Structure and Commercial Blight* (University of Chicago: Department of Geography Research Paper No. 85, 1963).

[6] Reino Helle, "Retailing in Northern Finland, Particularly by Mobile Shops," *Fennia*, Vol. 91 (1964). Detailed cost accounting of sample business firms is included in the study.

[7] Robert A. Murdie, "Cultural Differences in Consumer Travel," *Economic Geography*, Vol. 41 (July 1965), 211–33.

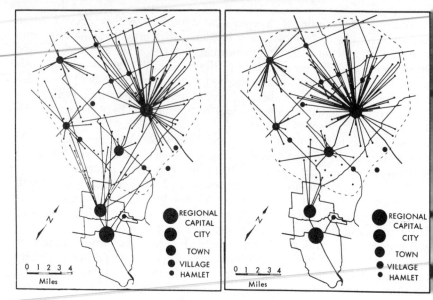

Fig. 5.1. *Banks used by "modern" Canadians (left) and Old Order Mennonites (right) in an area in Ontario.*

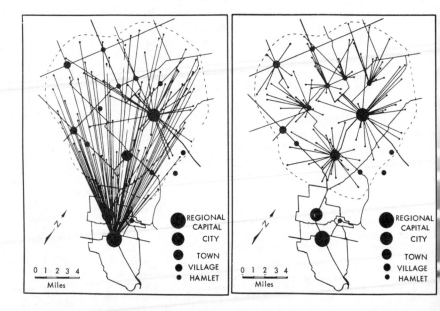

Fig. 5.2. *Towns visited for purchase of clothing (left) and yard goods (right) by "modern" Canadians and Mennonites.*

Mennonites behave like modern Canadians, no real differences in system use are seen, as in Figure 5.1, which shows where the modern Canadians (left) and Mennonites (right) use banks. However, where the traditional beliefs of the Mennonite group operate, two types of behavior are evident. Figure 5.2 shows where the modern Canadians purchase clothing (left) and the Mennonites buy their yard goods (right). The difference in transport technology is critical. Modern Canadians demand variety and have the opportunity to react to it, so the maximum distance they travel is related to size of center. The Mennonites, on the other hand, are restricted by use of horse and buggy, and buy only a limited variety of yard goods, so the maximum distance they travel does not vary with center size. See Figure 5.3.[8]

Periodic Markets in Peasant Societies

In most peasant societies, markets are periodic rather than permanent and continuous. The market is not open every day, but only once every

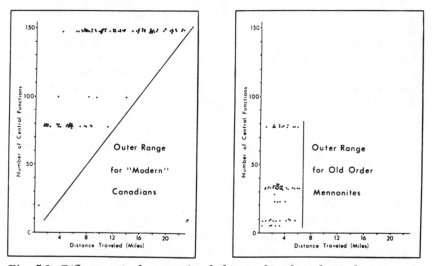

Fig. 5.3. Differences in the range for clothing and yard-goods purchase.

few days on a regularly scheduled basis, because the per capita demand for goods sold in the market is small, the market area is limited by primitive transport technology, and the aggregate demand is therefore insufficient to support permanent shops. Businessmen adjust by visiting several markets on a regular basis; and by accumulating the trade of several market areas they are able to survive.

[8] In his study, Murdie evaluates the main hypotheses about factors affecting consumer travel, and finds that size of center (and therefore variety of goods offered), socio-economic differences (determining the level of "space preference" of consumers —their personal predilections to assume particular levels of spatial interaction), and differences in the means and cost of transportation, are most important considerations.

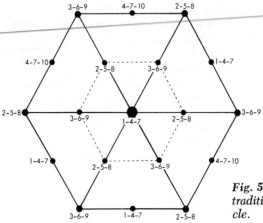

Fig. 5.4. *Periodicity of markets in a traditional Chinese 3-per-hsün cycle.*

Skinner's description of the periodic marketing system of traditional rural China may be used for exemplification, although details vary from one part of the world to another.[9] In supply, periodicity of the markets is related to the mobility of individual businessmen. The peddler toting his wares on a pole from one market to the next is the archetype of the mobile firm in China.[10] Equally characteristic is the wandering artisan or repairman, and itinerants purveying services from letter-writing to fortune-telling. From their point of view, periodic markets have the virtue of concentrating demand in specific places on specific days. When the firm is both producer and trader there are additional advantages, permitting sales and production to be undertaken on different days.

From the consumers' point of view, the periodicity of markets reduces the distance which must be traveled to obtain needed goods and services to a single day's excursion. Further, the subsistence production activities of the household can be combined with needed trips to the market.

The periodicities of individual markets are synchronized; Figure 5.4 depicts one such system recorded by Skinner. There are three levels of centers: standard markets, intermediate markets, and central markets, which are the highest order and are located at strategic points on the transport network, providing important wholesaling functions. The central market receives imported items and distributes them to its market area via the lower-order centers, and it collects local products and exports them to other central markets and higher-order centers. The standard market is the lowest-level central place, with the exception of minor "green vegetable markets," and meets periodically. The higher-level centers have permanent shops in addition to their periodic markets, and

[9] "Marketing and Social Structure in Rural China." The best statement linking periodic markets to central-place theory is that of James H. Stine, "Temporal Aspects of Tertiary Production Elements in Korea," in Forrest R. Pitts, ed., *Urban Systems and Economic Development* (Eugene: Univ. of Oregon, School of Business Administration, 1962), pp. 68–88. See also Belshaw, *Traditional Exchange and Modern Markets.*

[10] Compare with Helle, *op. cit.* and with Sven Dahl, "Travelling Pedlars in Nineteenth Century Sweden," *The Scandinavian Economic History Review,* Vol. 7 (1960), 167–78. Over much of the world the peddler is a woman—the "market mammies" of West Africa, or of Haiti; for example, see Belshaw, *op. cit.*

the central markets have smaller business centers at each of the four gates of the city, where the periodicity may even be on a twice-daily basis.[11]

The periodic marketing system of Figure 5.4 is one in which a merchant can move between the central market and a pair of standard markets in a ten-day cycle divided into units of three: the central market (day 1), first standard (2), second standard (3), central (4), first standard (5), second standard (6), central (7), first standard (8), second standard (9), and central on day 10, when no business is transacted. The interlocking periodicities of a large number of market centers of different levels can be seen in the figure. See also Figures 3.15 and 3.18.

Such cycles are determined either by "natural" means, using the motions of the heavenly bodies, or they are "artificial," without reference to any natural cycles. Ten-day marketing weeks were, for example, tied to the lunar month, whereas the seven-day marketing week of the Christian calendar is entirely artificial.

In China, the two fundamental cycles were the lunar decade (*hsün*), beginning on the first, eleventh, and twenty-first of each lunar month, and the 12-day duodenary cycle. Skinner argues that a *one per-hsün* cycle was originally adopted by the Chinese ancients in the valley of the Huang Ho, whereas a *one-per-duodenum* cycle was adopted in the southwest. As market systems developed, first the higher-level and finally the standard markets doubled their schedules, and later the highest-level centers doubled their schedules again.

---

[11] Skinner notes that there are two urban hierarchies in China. One is the system described above; the second is administrative, where cities are the centers of districts (*hsien*), prefectures (*fu*), or provinces (*sheng*), a hierarchy which corresponds to the tripartite administrative structure. The two hierarchies occasionally meet at the same level in the same cities, although this is not a necessity. Authors elsewhere have also pointed out a series of levels of periodic markets. In Northern Morocco, Mikesell recognizes two major types of markets. The local *suq* is the more influential and draws a few hundred people from a radius of 10 to 12 miles. Its primary function is to serve as focus of commerce for a dispersed but sedentary population engaged in subsistence agriculture. The second type is the *suq* which serves as a regional market, and draws a larger number of people from a radius of as much as 20 miles. Markets of this type are located at the convergence of major communication lines and on the frontiers of complementary production zones. Each of the markets has four major functions: (1) distribution of local products, (2) exchange of a rural surplus for urban goods, (3) circulation of articles such as pottery and millstones, and (4) dissemination for foreign imports. The larger regional *suq* differs from the local *suq* in its greater emphasis upon the last two functions. In Haiti, Mintz defines four major classes of markets: (1) strategic markets, (2) "captured" markets, (3) local markets, and (4) mixed markets. Strategic markets play a central role in the entire marketing system of Haiti. They bring local produce together for export, move staple crops to other regions and to the capital, serve as a "break-point" for staple crops from elsewhere in Haiti, and import goods for local consumption. Captured markets provision the local population of middle-class merchants and provide imported necessities to the peasants. They do not, however, provide bulking for other regions. Local markets are distinguished in that no subsidiary trading is produced by their existence. They are instead outlets for consumer goods via local exchange, and act as termini for broken-bulk imports and necessities originating in other areas. Mixed markets are primarily local markets, but attract some subsidiary trading activity. M. W. Mikesell, "The Role of Tribal Markets in Morocco," *Geographical Review*, Vol. 48 (October 1958), 494–511. S. W. Mintz, "A Tentative Typology of Eight Haitian Market Places," *Revista de Ciensios Sociales*, Vol. 4 (January 1960), 15–57.

One factor influencing the periodicity of markets is population density. Generally, the more people in the area, the greater the aggregate demand and the greater the frequency with which any market can meet, until, at the most frequent, it meets every day. Thus, periodic markets are logically related to the patterns observed in complex economies (Figure 2.10). A similar statement can be made about per capita demands as incomes rise or the peasant household begins to specialize more in production for sale: the more demands per capita increase, the greater the aggregate demand and periodicity, until permanency is achieved.

Across southern China, the periodicity of the duodenary cycle gradually increases from west to east, with the six-day week very common (1-7, 2-8, 3-9, 4-10, 5-11, and 6-12) and in the densest areas further doubling resulting in 1-4-7-10, 2-5-8-11, and 3-6-9-12. Across northern China, one-per-*hsün* cycles are found only in remote peripheral areas. Two-per-*hsün* cycles are the most common in standard markets, and four-per-*hsün* in central markets. The three-per-*hsün* schedules are common for standard markets in the regions of higher population densities at the heart of the Szechwan basin and the plains of southeastern China, and where densities are higher owing to specialization in food production for urban markets closer to big cities. Figures 5.4, 3.15, and 3.18 depict such three-per-*hsün* cycles.

Elsewhere in the world other cycles are found: two-per-*hsün* cycles are most common in Korea, whereas a one-per-*hsün* cycle was found in Japan prior to modernization. Both are presumably related to diffusion of Chinese culture in the north. In Rome, markets were held every ninth day. After the adoption of Christianity, the nine-day week was changed to a seven-day week and markets were held every Sunday. In time, clerical authorities became concerned with the worldliness of markets held about churches. In A.D. 906, for example, Sunday markets were prohibited in England. The weekday market which had sprung up, particularly in the trade of salt, iron, and local produce, took over the Sunday market functions. "Sunday towns" remain a common feature of life in Latin America even today, however, whereas "blue laws" and Sunday closing remain where Puritanical traditions are still strong.

Staggering of market days to facilitate both buyer and seller seems to be a nearly universal pattern. In Africa, the market week varies from a 3-day to a 7-day week. The 3-day, 4-day, 5-day, and 6-day weeks stem from ancient tribal differences, while the 7-day week resulted from calendar changes introduced by Islam into Africa.[12] In Kusai, the economy is oriented to a 3-day market cycle, and people think of three markets as being linked together. Each of these three markets is held on a consecutive day. Each, in turn, may be linked to another market cycle so that all of Kusai is covered by a connected net of market cycles. In

---

[12] A lengthy discussion of differences in market timing in Africa can be found in Willy Frohlich, "Das afrikanische Marktwesen," *Zeitschrift für Ethnologie*, Heft 1–3 (1940), 253–66. Polly Hill has termed the difference between West Africa, with its well-developed network of pre-European markets, and East Africa, which was without them, "one of the great geographical dichotomies of Africa." See "Markets in Africa," *Journal of Modern African Studies*, Vol. 1 (December 1963), 447.

Yorubaland, the markets operate on a ring system. Each ring is composed of a 4-day cycle or multiples of it. This timing is related to the former 4-day week in West Africa. Similar periodicities have been noted in India, and in Central and South America.

The standard marketing systems of China are shown by Skinner to be not simply exchange mechanisms, but the basic building-blocks of that society. Other authors imply the same for other societies.[13] Each standard market and its surrounding tributary area functions as an economic and social community, incorporating, on the average, 18 villages (Fig. 3.19).

Typically, one out of five adults living in the villages went to market on a market day in traditional China, to shop in the standard market in a multitude of petty market places, one for each product. This specialization is true elsewhere, and Figure 5.5 reproduces Fogg's diagram of the

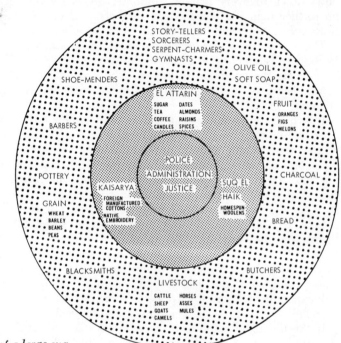

Fig. 5.5. Plan of a large suq.

structure of a large *suq* in Morocco. The market serves as a place for the peasant to sell what he produces and purchase what he needs. For both buyer and seller, a profit motive dominates; bargaining and haggling may be intense, even though monetary standards of exchange exist. Local credit societies exist for villages within the system; landlords collect their rents and transport coolies can be hired there. In turn, each standard market links into higher-level market systems. The local elite patronize

[13] Mikesell, for example, relates individual *suqs* or groups of *suqs* to particular tribes in Northern Morocco. Belshaw also points out the important role of market centers in social relations. The interest of American rural sociologists such as G. J. Galpin in central-place systems was basically because lower levels defined rural "neighborhoods" and "communities."

the intermediate and central markets, purchasing luxuries unavailable to the peasantry in standard markets. Further, traders return to their bases to replenish stocks or dispose of purchases. Even at the higher levels, peddlers selling less frequently demanded goods can be found in the central markets.

The whole is thus an interdependent system, with exotic goods sold in the central market and itinerants circulating in lower-level markets. Merchandise produced in the central towns is distributed downwards by the itinerants. Both central and intermediate towns have a variety of producer-distributor and wholesale-retail relationships in addition to their retailing functions. The intermediate towns generally include only distributors, whereas the central markets have wholesalers with warehouses. Merchandise consumed by the peasantry or required by petty craftsmen flows down to every market, consumer goods for the local elite move no further than the intermediate markets, and consumer goods for the bureaucratic elite, and industrial supplies, never leave the central markets.

The upward flow of goods begins with the peasant selling his produce to local consumers or to dealers who process and/or bulk the product. These pass the goods on to buyers, who carry them to intermediate or central markets, and perhaps up through successively higher levels of centers.

In what ways are the standard market communities social systems? They are endogamous for the peasantry; marriage brokers arrange marriages between villages within them. Leading shopkeepers and the local elite form committees responsible for the local religious festival. Voluntary and formal organizations use the standard marketing community as their unit of organization (for example, the composite lineage, the secret-society lodge, the committee arranging the local fair, the religious service society). Local variants of these elements of social integration repeat themselves elsewhere in the world. If a world map differentiating countries by level of economic development is examined, for example that in Wilbur Zelinsky's companion volume in this series,[14] those parts of the world considered "underdeveloped" or with "isolated tribal economies" will generally be found to have periodic marketing systems in which basic economic units and basic social units are identical.

If the details of periodicity, commodities traded, and forms of social integration vary culturally, so do the locations of periodic markets. All locate to serve both buyers and sellers efficiently, but sites selected may differ among cultures. Most commonly, markets locate at crossroads and space themselves in a manner determined by the maximum distances consumers are willing to walk. The spacing is affected but little after an early period of development by differences in population density; instead, the periodicity of the markets adjusts as densities change, to serve increased demands by increased meetings. In Morocco, siting is determined by locations of springs and wells, to provide a reliable water supply, preferably close to a religious sanctuary or shrine, to guarantee

[14] *A Prologue to Population Geography*, pp. 94–95.

protection. Larger *suqs* locate on the boundaries between production zones. In many places, for example, Yorubaland, and in North Africa, the rural population lives away from the market sites, and the hierarchy of rural settlements is not related to the hierarchy of periodic markets. This phenomenon also persists in Eastern Europe. Elsewhere, however, rural settlements and periodic markets coincide. At this level few generalizations can be made. After general system-properties of periodic markets have been outlined, an understanding of local variability must be embedded in an understanding of local culture.

Fairs

Fairs complement periodic markets in peasant economies, but whereas periodic markets are chiefly agencies for satisfying local demand, fairs meet less frequently, reflect regional differences in economic activity, and attract buyers from distant areas by virtue of their specialization. If the Latin roots of the word *market* refer to both the act of exchange and the place where exchange is transacted, the term *fair* derives from roots meaning a celebration or festival.

In the most ambitious attempt at comparative investigation of fairs, limited to the Old World, Allix distinguishes among four analogous institutions—the general commodity fair, the livestock fair, the country market, and the sample fair.[15] The *commodity fair* represented the sole mechanism of large-scale commerce in a state of civilization with no security for regular exchange and limited means of transportation.[16] In many societies, exchange occurred on neutral ground during a period of truce. Historically, much of the commerce in these societies was *Grenzhandel,* or frontier commerce.

Allix feels that the fair arose from caravan transport as well as frontier commerce. In North Africa, the fair grew out of the gatherings for trade at the "ports" of caravans. The caravans eventually found it in their self-interest to arrive at the time of festivals, so fairs had a timing related to religious events.

The *livestock fair* appears superficially to be a derivative of the commodity fair, but in reality is an independent institution. Perhaps the most ancient type of fair and probably the most persistent, its origins were in the rural countryside. Agriculture, by its nature, imposes intermittency upon commercial gatherings, which are most often periodic for convenience. In a sedentary agricultural population, these gatherings can be held at frequent intervals. In pastoral nomadism, however, the interval is related to progression of the seasons and movement of the herds, so the

[15] Andre Allix, "The Geography of Fairs: Illustrated by Old World Examples," *Geographical Review,* Vol. 12 (October 1922), 532–69.

[16] Such an example were the *mouggars* held on the Saharan fringe. Before the coming of the French they were the only times when exchange could take place with assurance of life and property, and they served as the intermediaries of commercial life between the Sahara, the Sudan, and Morocco. Walter Fogg, "The Suq: A Study in the Human Geography of Morocco," *Geography,* Vol. 17 (November 1932), 257–58.

gatherings attain particular importance at certain seasons of the year; thus the livestock fair is born.[17]

Allix goes on to point out that these rural gatherings were nearly always held in the open country in the beginning, but with time tended to become fixed centers of habitation. This concentration of agricultural exchange in the form of a *country market* is one of the reasons urban settlements come about. As the town develops, it begins to acquire its own proper functions, and ends by absorbing all the country products. Thus, the city market arises.

The final major form of fair that Allix recognizes is the *sample fair*. By 1897, when the Leipzig fair had declined to a point where its very existence was imperiled, an effort was made to preserve the wholesale trade of the fair and prevent degeneration into a local retail fair. Since the old system was incompatible with direct bulk sales, the idea of sale with immediate delivery was abandoned. Instead, visitors and buyers were offered only samples of merchandise and orders were taken. In this way, merchandise was exchanged from buyer to seller without passing through the fair.

Timing of fairs is complex. The temporal sequence in fair activity often involves seasonal fluctuation in the number of fairs, with changes in fair specialization reflecting variations in products available in surrounding producing regions. Because of these seasonal changes, the activity of fairs often shows a spatial sequence related to the growing season and climate. Furthermore, the duration of any single fair is often itself divided into times when special products or economic activity predominate.

Kniffen, in his study of the American agricultural fair, finds that it is closely akin to the ancient harvest festival and traditionally comes in autumn.[18] This association has become so deeply impressed upon the American mind that many are unaware that fairs occur in other seasons. Yet, American colonial market fairs commonly had a spring session, and specialty fairs for livestock, poultry, and citrus fruit were not so restricted.

For each general region of the United States, Kniffen found a recognized fair season, progressing from the earliest fair held near the Canadian border to those of the last of the year in the southern states. He mapped all the accurately known circuits for 1949, noting that organized circuits are restricted to areas where fairs are numerous and horse-racing a prominent part of the fair.

The association of each fair with a particular calendar week becomes strongly established. On the whole, the common duration for a fair is six days, Monday through Saturday. Within this fair week, one day—usually Thursday—is traditionally more important than the others.

---

[17] Fogg argues that this second type generally becomes an *annual fair*, and in many cases developed out of the possibilities of exchange where a large number of people gathered together in the name of a particular saint. Their influence may be quite local, as in the many religious festivals of India, or may have very wide appeal and be attended by thousands.

[18] Fred Kniffen, "The American Agricultural Fair: The Pattern," *Annals*, Association of American Geographers, Vol. 39 (December 1949), 264–82, and "The American Agricultural Fair: Time and Place," *ibid.*, Vol. 41 (March 1951), 42–57.

In the Central Andes of South America, there is also a marked seasonal distribution of fairs. Most fairs take place at the change of season. No fairs of importance are held in January, February, or March, when the rainy season is at its height. This seasonal variation has a religious explanation. To the Peruvians, the seasons of germination and maturity are marked by spiritual recognition. They are times of ceremony, when the entire agricultural community comes together. The fair, originally primarily of a religious character, grew into a more mercantile enterprise. Similar examples can be cited throughout the world.

Periodicity, the most obvious trait of commodity fairs, conceals a more fundamental characteristic—the itinerant nature of traders and their merchandise. The merchant is able to travel from fair to fair only by the combination of dates and rhythms of the various fairs. Thus, the trader at fairs repeats on a larger scale the behavior of the peddler in the periodic market.

Allix demonstrates the intimate connection between the livestock fair and pastoral life. In pastoral nomadism, the fair is a permanent element of both economic and social structure. Since herdsmen are accustomed to meeting other herdsmen at fixed intervals, exchange of animals, making contracts for engagement of herdsmen, and sale of pastoral produce becomes commonplace, giving rise to the cattle fair. It represents the sole commercial outlet for the pastoral region, and the sole economic contact of the pastoral region with the exterior. In addition, since it is the only chance for the pastoral people to buy products of everyday need, the cattle fair is almost always accompanied by a certain amount of general merchandise and is attended by a host of itinerant retail traders. There is an indissoluble connection between the rhythm of the fairs and that of pastoral nomadism. The tenacity of this connection is illustrated by the abortive attempt during the French Revolution to change the traditional dates of fairs.

Like periodic markets, fairs show an internal grouping of products. This is particularly true for the general commodity fair, with diverse products localized within the fair, but also usually applies to the livestock fair. Internal division facilitates transactions, since consumer movements and confusion are kept at a minimum.

There is a complexity in fair location equal to that of periodic markets. Some factors differ in influence or in kind among cultures; other variables remain important throughout most peasant societies.

Fairs were most often held on boundaries in neutral lands where rival tribes could meet to trade. In ancient Italy, for example, one of the most important fairs was held on a boundary which separated Etruscan from Sabine lands. In Greece, markets were held on boundaries under the protection of gods of the Agora. Irish fairs were frequently held in or near cemeteries, while similar sites at churchyards can be found in England. English fairs were often held on hilltops—St. Giles Hill Fair, Weyhill Fair, and the fair at St. Ann's Hill are examples. There was a close connection between hilltop fairs and ancient trackways.

In the United States, Kniffen points out that, while the chief function of market fairs is commercial, the agricultural fair is educational, so different considerations enter into its location. The educational American county fair is a quasi-governmental institution, and therefore normally situated at the county seat. The state fair is usually held in the capital or largest city. Transportation is an important locational factor. In pre-automobile days, some local fairs were accessible only with horse and buggy; those attending larger fairs came chiefly by rail. Today, the automobile is the chief form of transportation. The fairgrounds commonly lie at the edge of the community. Although there have been some cases where fairs are surrounded by an expanding city, few manage to survive the economic competition. The fair must have, for its site, a good water supply and flat terrain for buildings and the race-track; it profits from a grove of trees to shade picnickers and trailer living quarters.

In the Central Andes, fairs were located at some equating point for the movement of products and people. Several were situated in the Titicaca Basin between the Peruvian valleys and the Argentine pampas, the rich valleys of the montana and the coastal ports. Other equating points were on the borders of well-marked natural regions.

In Elizabethan England, distribution of long and recurrent fairs was closely associated with eastern and western ports of entry into England by sea, and with the commercial "boundary" between northeast and southwest. On this boundary traders evidently found an almost continuous market throughout the year. This was the location at which foreign merchants could hope to find a relatively constant demand for continental goods and luxuries. Long and recurrent fairs were also located at well-defined road intersections or near some recognized line of travel. Many of the great fair towns of England lay along the road from London through Leicester to Manchester. Even the variable of road transportation, however, fails to account for a significant number of important fairs and fair clusters. Only when the fair distribution is compared with a map of Roman communications are these "roadless" centers of trade brought into relation with lines of transport. The Roman roads which rationalize the position of important or minor fair sites were still in use during the Elizabethan period, together with many trackways.

Allix reiterates the importance of the great highways of communication to the location of fairs. A map viewing a country's fairs at their time of apogee will show them on the great trade routes of the time. Ordinarily, Allix notes, two classes of circumstances favor the location of fairs. First, they may be located in the centers of producing regions. The Flemish fairs were essentially the outlet of the 17 cloth-manufacturing towns which, in the Middle Ages, made Flanders the first textile region of the continent. Second, fairs might have a location at places of transit and at crossroads. This is exemplified by the frontier locations of Champagne, Breslau, and the two Frankforts. When these two locational factors can be combined—the producing region and the crossing of great highways—the conditions are exceptional for making a fortune in the manner of a Lyons or a Leipzig.

Allix goes on to examine the importance of settlement to fairs, pointing out that fairs are often held outside towns in the open country. It may be, as at Timbuktu, that the town is an isolated point of fixed habitation around which nomad life is centered, in which case fairs may give rise to fixed centers of population or greatly encourage their growth. When there is a superimposition of fair and town, the institutions are essentially distinct. Allix notes that great fairs have often been long associated with small towns, as was the case at Beaucaire in southern France near the mouth of the Rhone, at Briancon, the frontier town of the French Alps on the great road to Italy, and at St. Denis, near Paris. Undoubtedly the towns do derive some benefit from the fair, but less than is commonly thought. The town treasury and inns gain the most, while local trade scarcely profits at all. The fair greatly increases the population, but only momentarily. The fair is of a nature entirely different from that of the town, with which it has only superficial relations. These conclusions were reiterated by Pirenne in his history of Europe.[19]

Reciprocal and Redistributive Exchange in the Simplest Societies

Men have a variety of wants in any society—for food, clothing, shelter, prestige, and social standing; as producers they work to satisfy these wants. Economic systems develop out of the need for some form of organization to ensure that demands are met by production of the proper kinds and quantities of supplies.

Consider Robinson Crusoe. Responsible for satisfying all his own demands, he decided what he wanted, had to *extract* his raw materials and crops, *transport* them to his workshops, *process* them to create desired products, *store* the products at some convenient place until the need for them arose, and finally *distribute* them in proper proportions to the spots where they would finally be consumed. His *productive process* (embodying the stages of extraction, processing, and distribution, and the attendant operations of transportation and storage) thus led to final satisfaction of his needs in *consumption*.

Crusoe is a complete *economic system* unto himself, for he originates the *demands*, creates the *supplies*, and so organizes his work that his demands and supplies are maintained in over-all equilibrium.

Crusoe's little economic system also has important geographic (spatial) characteristics, for it is a rare man who, like the angels of medieval scholasticism, can exist on the head of a pin. He must of necessity carry out his productive enterprises in different locations which, presumably, balance excellence for the particular enterprise with the need to keep over-all effort devoted to work reasonably small. Crusoe might, for example, visit the third-ranking fishing spot instead of the first or second, because the two better spots involve extra travel time and effort more profitably devoted to alternative activities like farming and hunting. His economic system is also, therefore, a geographic system or *space-economy* in which relative advantages of different locations and costs of transporting goods are balanced to keep expenditure of effort down while satisfying demands.

[19] Henri Pirenne, *Economic and Social History of Medieval Europe* (New York: Harcourt, 1936), pp. 98–100.

Robinson Crusoes are found in abundance today only in elementary economics textbooks, for men are by nature social animals clustering together in communities of varying sizes. Both historically, and in the less "westernized" parts of the world today, however, examples may be found of communities with simple, Crusoe-like economic systems. These are self-sustaining communities in which the proper quantities and varieties of products are distributed to consumers without the need for even periodic markets.

In Crusoe's case the decision as to how much to produce and how to distribute the output was his own *individual* one. In Crusoe-like economies the decision is *social;* the rules, obligations, traditions, and group decisions of the community determine who shall produce what and how it will be distributed.

Three patterns of social control have been identified among the many subsistence economies that have been studied (largely by anthropologists): *householding, redistribution,* and *reciprocity.*

Householding is a literal translation of the Greek word *oeconomia,* the etymon for our word "economy." A more appropriate rendering of the meaning is "production for one's own use," or, as the economic historian Karl Polanyi has expressed it, "whether the different entities of the family or the settlement or the manor form the self-sufficient unit, the principle is invariably the same: that of producing and storing for the satisfaction of the wants of the members of the group. . . . Production for use as against production for gain is the essence of householding." [20]

The householding unit is a self-sustaining entity, an independent cell. The medieval *manor,* the Roman *familia,* and the South Slav *zadruga* were comparable householding economic systems. Large numbers of such independent economic units were the bases of feudal society in Europe, to cite one example of the cellular societies that have characterized the world.

In its pattern and organization, the householding unit is closest to Robinson Crusoe. Instead of the single consumer there are several members of the household; instead of the single producer there are several, with division of labor based upon age, sex, social standing, and tradition. The function of the distribution system is to gather the output of specialist producers who, by virtue of specialization, have become mutually interdependent, and deposit it at the place or places where members of the household will consume it.

The medieval manor comprised a series of families who worked cooperatively in cultivating their communal fields, woods, pastures, and ponds. But each family had an established right to the output from certain strips of land, to pasture a certain number of animals, to use a certain amount of wood, and so forth. Equity was maintained by these rights.

---

[20] Karl Polanyi, *Trade and Markets in the Early Empires* (Glencoe: Free Press, 1957); and *The Great Transformation* (New York: Rinehart, 1944). See also Philip L. Wagner, *The Human Use of the Earth* (Glencoe: Free Press, 1960); and Cyril S. Belshaw, *Traditional Exchange and Modern Markets* (Englewood Cliffs: Prentice-Hall, 1965).

Distribution served each family in the simple way that it served Crusoe.[21]

There are certain societies in which equity is maintained through the institution of a strong central authority, whose function is redistributive. Goods are, upon production, delivered to this headman, then parceled out by him to members of the social group in ways determined by custom. Many of the ancient empires, such as the New Kingdom of Egypt, were founded upon this principle of redistribution. It is also common among many of the cattle-raising tribes of East Africa. One interesting manifestation is found in the *potlatch* of the *Kwakiutl* of the Pacific Northwest, in which the chief assembled the wealth of the tribe and redistributed it by giving to others in elaborate ceremonies, with the ultimate objective of making the receiver the social debtor, and ultimately the retainer.

The third pattern is reciprocity in the assurance of needed exchange. An example will illustrate. In the Trobriand Islands of Western Melanesia (studied by Malinowski), inland communities are paired with coastal villages in a pattern of exchange of inland breadfruits for coastal fish. The pairing extends to particular individuals being responsible for the direct exchange, in symmetrical arrangements of remarkable regularity and persistence. Many such exchanges are often disguised in the form of reciprocal giving-of-gifts, but the principle is no less effective.

Karl Polanyi, whose impressive and massive work of synthesis is responsible for current understanding of the subordination of primitive economic life to social rules and traditions, describes the essence of the three patterns well. He argues that all economic systems known up to the end of feudalism in Western Europe were organized either on the principles of reciprocity, redistribution, or householding, or on some combination of the three. The orderly production and distribution of goods was secured through a great variety of individual motives disciplined by general principles of behavior. Gain was not prominent among these motives. Custom and law, magic and religion, cooperated in inducing the individual to comply with the rules of behavior which, eventually, ensured his functioning in the economic system. Further, Polanyi argues that as long as social organization runs in ruts, no individual economic motives need come into play; no shirking of personal effort need be feared; division of labor will automatically be ensured; economic obligations will be duly discharged; and material means for an excellent display of abundance at all public festivals will be ensured. Such are the simplest forms of exchange, not simply in feudal Europe, but in all societies in which the market place is absent.

---

[21] See for relevant discussions "Morphogenesis of the Agrarian Cultural Landscape," *Geografiska Annaler*, Vol. 43 (1961), Nos. 1–2. In one paper in this collection, Glanville Jones points out that the basic social and territorial unit of organization in Britain was a grouping of hamlets, known as a *maenor*, under the authority of a lord. This unit was self-sustaining. See "Early Territorial Organization in England and Wales," pp. 174–81.

CHAPTER SIX

Paths to the present:
theory and fact

The market arrangements of different cultures are not distinct, but related in a developmental sequence. This chapter discusses the transformation from each stage of the sequence to the next, and changes taking place within each of the stages.

Market centers emerged only after goods began to move to consumers in exchange systems transcending the limits of the householding unit or the immediate social group, replacing the management of exchange by reciprocity or redistribution. Two possible sources of the change have been identified. One involved the emergence of periodic markets in systems of local trade, the other the establishment of fairs along long-distance trade routes. Both of these should be distinguished from central-place hierarchies in complex modern economies. Neither local nor long-distance trade disturbed the subsistence base of the householding units in peasant societies. The role of modern central-place hierarchies is, on the other hand, predicated upon extreme division of labor and the absence of household self-sufficiency in necessities.

A three-stage sequence is thus envisioned. The first involves socially administered exchange. In the second, barter and, later, money provided the standards of value permitting market-place transactions in peasant societies. Finally, the peasant dualism between subsistence and trade has been replaced in some parts of the world by the specialization of modern economies, and periodic markets and fairs by a highly articulated array of market centers. The series of revolutions (industrial, commercial, agricultural, political) involved in what Polanyi calls "The Great Transformation" [1] all led toward increasing specialization and the breakdown of local self-sufficiency. Places and social units in ever widening areas began to depend on others for sustenance. To make sure that demands and supplies

---

[1] In his book of the same title (New York: Rinehart, 1944).

were in balance, the distribution system assumed a more fundamental role, and a whole range of market centers emerged to ensure that consumers would be supplied with correct quantities and types of goods and services at the proper time.

Emergence of Local and Long-Distance Trade

Perhaps the earliest long-distance trade was exploration beyond the limits of the local area. Such exploration might involve warlike forays or irregular trading, often for ritual goods associated with the god-king and the temple, the focus of society and social controls.[2] So long as the resulting exchange of goods was sporadic, market centers did not develop. Only when regular trade connections emerged was there justification for establishment of permanent market places.

One regular form of long-distance exchange was between complementary production zones, for example, between plains dwellers and hill folk, each trading surpluses of their own specialty for those of the other. Market sites would often develop along the territorial boundary zone, on neutral ground. At the appropriate season, often in conjunction with religious festivities, people from surrounding areas would converge upon the market sites to barter surpluses. Where relations between the different groups were strained, such times would also be those of truce.

Market centers also developed at stopping places on the great trade routes of the world, such as the silk routes between China and Europe. Fords, riverheads, ports, other points of transshipment, and the ends of routes, became logical places for exchange to take place.

Most luxuries and trinkets found their way from these exchange-points to the peasants at great seasonal festivals. The festivals originated as religious celebrations, but soon developed commercial sidelines which became their *raison d'être*. Only a few of the lighter, more expensive items of dress, personal adornment, and spices for the elite, ritual materials required for religious purposes, and metal implements, salt, and trinkets used by all classes came from outside. Often the sources of these things were at tremendous distances.

Local trade emerged on the basis of regular intercourse between peasants, local craftsmen and specialists, and town merchants and middlemen. Local surpluses would be traded for such necessities as salt, iron, or durables, and merchants would have available some luxuries and trinkets obtained from the great fairs. To fit in with work on the land, the markets would be held periodically. Links connecting long-distance trade, the great fairs, and local periodic markets were provided by the town merchants.

Neither local nor long-distance trade appear to have been responsible for the growth of cities. Periodic markets and fairs still meet on ground where there is no permanent settlement. Market centers are among the main reasons for cities in complex modern economies, however, and although there are other reasons for cities (notably specialization in

[2] Robert McC. Adams, *The Evolution of Urban Society* (Chicago: Aldine, 1966).

mining, or industrial production), there are never markets without an associated urban center. Thus Christaller formulated central-place theory as concerning both retail location and urban location.

The earliest cities were associated, in subsistence societies, with growth of an urban community around, and initially dependent upon, a palace and/or a temple, located within a citadel or stronghold. Such cities, performing political, military, religious, or administrative roles, were not integral parts of society; a clear separation between the urban and the rural existed—a dualism far sharper than that between the subsistence and trading facets of peasant societies. Such cities drew their requirements from the surrounding countryside, either by force of arms or some socially determined pattern of redistribution (for example, by maintaining the Pharaoh's grain warehouses in the New Kingdom of Egypt, by the lord receiving his feudal due in medieval Europe, or by tithing to the Christian church), but returned very little to it.

With the emergence of local and long-distance trade and the dualism of peasant societies, market sites and trading posts became widespread, but most of these sites were occupied for marketing purposes only periodically. Local trade in particular provided no basis for growth of cities, even if surpluses obtained at the weekly markets did augment the urban food supply. Although grants of market-rights and coinage to owners of strongholds were made as early as the ninth or tenth centuries in Europe, these functions were carried on inside the stronghold and did not lead to growth of urban communities outside its walls. On the other hand, the combination of a stronghold or temple with a great fair on a major trade route often did lead to the emergence of great cities. Pirenne related the regeneration of urbanism in Europe after the Dark Ages to the rebirth of trade.

A debate now wages between two theories of the origins of periodic markets and fairs. The first, dating at least from Adam Smith's *Wealth of Nations*,[3] starts with an agrarian society in which surpluses develop, permitting a basic form of division of labor to emerge from the propensity of individuals to barter the surpluses, and leads to the establishment of a specialist group of artificers (smiths, carpenters, wheelwrights) located in a village central to the farmers they serve and with whom they exchange. The village becomes the most convenient site for trade between the cultivators, too, and assumes the status of a periodic market. Specialization then proceeds further, and additional surpluses lead to interregional trade, especially in crude manufactures using the region's resources. Since the manufacturers have urban locations, an important element of interregional trade is interurban. Ultimately, a hierarchy of urban centers with marketing functions develops, to mediate local, intraregional, interregional, and interurban trade. The sequence is one of a propensity and ability to barter; local exchange, division of labor, and markets; and external exchange and markets. Thus, one source argues

---

[3] *An Inquiry into the Nature and Causes of the Wealth of Nations*, 1776. See pp. 356–96 of the Modern Library edition, ed. Edwin Cannon (New York, 1937).

. . . barter exists among the most isolated and inaccessible societies; and the wordless exchange of goods made without witness in the furthermost recesses of the jungle, in Asia, America and Africa is evidence of an economic need. As confidence grows between individuals exchanging their respective goods, local markets spring up; and in the more advanced cultures wide use may be made of money in the more important markets or regional fairs.[4]

The alternative view stems from the work of Polanyi and Pirenne,[5] and reverses the sequence, stating that trade and markets can never arise within communities, for trade is external, involving different communities. Markets do not develop out of the demands of purely local or individual commerce, but are primarily induced by external exchanges of complementary products with an alien population, and are thus the result rather than the starting point of long-distance trading. The sequence is seen as one of trade routes, fairs established on these routes, and local (periodic) markets developing around the original parent market as a network of tracks or roads spreads.

Hodder reviews evidence for and against the two views in Africa.[6] In Yorubaland, the evidence in support of the second theory seems overwhelming. The earliest markets located along the contact zone between forest and savanna, along coastal lagoons and creeks, or at the boundaries between different peoples. More important, the larger markets were along the chief trade routes, and changed in importance with these routes. One important origin of Yoruba markets was the resting place where local populations provided services to passing groups of traders. If such resting places became popular, a market into which farmers brought their wares for sale sprang up, and periodic market days developed. Extra large meetings would be held less frequently, when large numbers of traders converged.

The essence of the traditional view is identity between the processes of urban development and growth of market centers in an evolutionary sequence. But in Yorubaland locations of periodic markets and of settlements diverged. Traditional markets were true central places, foci of communication, not nuclei of settlement. This is to be expected when markets originate in external contacts rather than by natural development within a given social context.

To follow Hodder's survey further, although he emphasizes the fragmentary nature of the evidence, the materials available suggest growth out of long-distance trading contacts in the majority of West African communities. The same story is repeated for Ethiopia and the Horn of Africa, for the contacts of Kikuyu, Masai, Kamba, Arab, and Swahili in East Africa, further south with the Bantu, and in the Congo.

---

[4] International Labour Organization, "Indian Markets and Fairs in Latin America," in *Indigenous Peoples*, 1953, quoted in B. W. Hodder, "Some Comments on the Origins of Traditional Markets in Africa South of the Sahara," *Transactions of the Institute of British Geographers*, Vol. 36 (1965), 97–105.

[5] H. Pirenne, *Economic and Social History of Medieval Europe* (New York: Harcourt, 1936).

[6] *Op. cit.*

In southern and southeastern Africa, on the other hand, there is no evidence of the existence of periodic markets. The markets found there today are of recent origin, introduced by Europeans or other outside groups, although there is some evidence of barter.[7] Lack of periodic markets is explained by isolation of the most primitive subsistence societies from the main interregional trade routes. If there was internal exchange, it never gave rise to markets, but remained as reciprocal gift-giving, as, for example, among the Bulu of Cameroun.

Hodder argues that without two additional conditions opportunities presented by long-distance external trading contacts can never be grasped and channeled through market institutions. The first is a sufficiently high level of population density. Below about 50 persons per square mile, there are not enough people within walking distance of any central point to justify a market or to permit much economic diversification among individuals. Second, only where well-developed and highly organized political units existed could communities profit from trading possibilities; without strong political organization, security of markets could not be ensured. These ideas are reiterated by Adams in his studies of the ritual bases of urban origins and long-distance trade.[8]

The dilemma posed by Hodder, and the impressive fund of evidence he assembles in support of the non-traditional view, parallels exactly the trend of arguments concerning urban origins in America and the role of urban centers in the development of the American market economy. The traditional views are those of Turner and Gras.[9]

Turner argued that the continent was occupied in a series of waves.

It begins with the Indian and the hunter; it goes on to tell of the disintegration of savagery by the entrance of the trader, the pathfinder of civilization; we read the annals of the pastoral stage in ranch life; the exploitation of the soil by the raising of unrotated crops of corn and wheat in sparsely settled farming communities; the extensive culture of the denser farm settlement; and finally the manufacturing organization with city and factory system.

In this evolutionary scheme, market towns developed as the frontier of commercial agriculture passed over lands previously transformed by passage of a frontier of peasant farmers.

Gras's thesis involved a more global view of five stages of economic evolution: collectional economy, cultural nomadic economy, settled village economy, town economy, and metropolitan economy. Market centers

---

[7] See, for example, Paul Bohannan and George Dalton, *Markets in Africa* (Evanston: Northwestern Univ., 1962).

[8] *The Evolution of Urban Society.*

[9] F. J. Turner, "The Significance of the Frontier in American History," in *The Turner Thesis Concerning the Role of the Frontier in American History,* a volume in *Problems in American Civilization,* ed. G. R. Taylor (Boston: Heath, 1956); A. M. Schlesinger, "The City in American Civilization," in *Paths to the Present* (New York: Macmillan, 1949), pp. 210–33; N. S. B. Gras, *An Introduction to Economic History* (New York: Harper, 1922); and "The Development of Metropolitan Economy in Europe and America," *American Historical Review,* Vol. 27 (July 1922), 695–708.

developed in the settled village stage, and subsequent stages added to the complexity of the urban hierarchy. In the final stage, the metropolis organizes the market, leads the processes of industrial development and transportation, and moulds the pattern of financial organization.

Wade's more recent argument [10] in tracing the rise of the Old West is: "The towns were the spearheads of the frontier. Planted far in advance of the line of settlement, they held the West for the approaching population." He cites the insights of Josiah Strong: "In the Middle States the farms were first taken, then the town sprang up to supply its wants, and at length the railway connected it with the world; but in the West the order is reversed—first the railroad, then the towns, then the farms. Settlement is, consequently, much more rapid, and the city stamps the country, instead of the country stamping the city." [11]

Our evidence on the development of market centers in southwestern Iowa supports the views of Wade and the insights of Strong. The non-traditional view of emergence of markets out of external contacts appears to have priority.

Change in Peasant Marketing

Two major sources of change exist within peasant marketing systems —increasing population densities and increasing household participation in the marketing process. The former initially had priority, whereas under the pressures of modernization the second is the main source of change today.

Skinner relates the results of changing population densities in China: initially, new markets would be established and existing markets grow; next, the size of markets continues to grow, but larger ones add new dates to their periodic schedules, within the framework of a given set of centers; finally, markets stabilize and periodicity vanishes, except perhaps on a diurnal basis. Further increases in population density are accompanied by increases in the number and decreases in the spacing of permanent market centers. Total volumes of trade increase, as do the numbers of marketing hours per week. Permanent firms replace their mobile counterparts, and the degree and scope of economic specialization widens.

The working of this process in India has led Singh to formulate a *stability theory* of central-place development,[12] relating to central places serving as centers for small rural regions as nuclei of exchange and barter, places of entertainment, worship, and social interaction. He shows age of market in the Faizabad district to be related to size of center, and tabulates the activity in the weekly cycle (Fig. 6.1). In the smallest markets there are one or two meetings per week; permanent shops are absent

---

[10] Richard C. Wade, *The Urban Frontier* (Cambridge: Harvard Univ., 1959).

[11] Strong, *Our Country: Its Possible Future and Its Present Crisis* (New York: Baker and Taylor, 1885), p. 206.

[12] Shiw Mangal Singh, "The Stability Theory of Rural Central Place Development," *The National Geographical Journal of India*, Vol. 11 (March 1965), 13–21. See also Stine's work in Korea, in Pitts, ed., *Urban Systems and Economic Development*.

from the market site. On market day 75 per cent of the sellers are peasant producers, not middlemen; foodstuffs and handicrafts are the main items traded. Itinerant tradesmen called *khochiwalas* walk from one such market to another in a weekly cycle. In larger, older centers the numbers of permanent shops managed by middlemen increase, along with wholesalers and small credit institutions. The final stage is stability.

Skinner also relates the changes that took place in China as peasant households were linked to growing urban markets for food and handicrafts, and to urban sources of exotic goods. In the traditional hierarchy of markets in China, successively higher levels of center were characterized by greater volumes of trade, more marketing hours per week, higher proportions of permanent to mobile firms, and a greater degree and scope of economic specialization. Traditional change involved extension of the characteristics to lower-level centers as population densities increased. Modernization involves gradual commercialization of the agrarian economy, however, and increases in the marketing done by the household, thus proceeding from two bases: extension of urban demands into the countryside, and rapid contraction of household self-sufficiency. Marketing systems within the city's trading area are commercialized, and the system of periodic markets is transformed into a stable central-place hierarchy.

The interlocked industrial, urban, and agricultural revolutions of the past three centuries can, in this sense, be seen as the reason for the articulated provision of retail and service business in an urban hierarchy and the emergence of such an urban hierarchy out of early systems of fairs and periodic markets. Colonial penetration has been a similar source of change in peasant societies elsewhere, and commercial transformation of markets established or influenced by colonial administration or economic penetration is a source of further social change in peasant

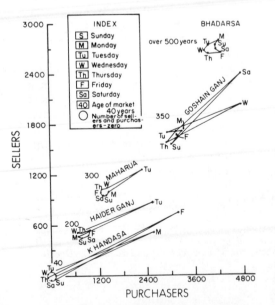

Fig. 6.1. *Age, size, and periodicity of bazaars in Faizabad area, India.*

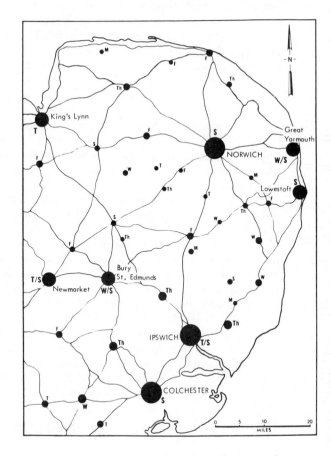

Fig. 6.2. Market days in East Anglia.

households.[13] The countries of Western Europe, with a long history of modernization, have vestigial traces of earlier fairs and market periodicities that characterized their peasant state, in the market days of country towns, while lands newly settled in the past three centuries in the New World and southern hemisphere have purely "modern" urban hierarchies. Thus, in England "market day" remains a residual feature of rural life (Fig. 6.2), as do less frequent fairs. Local markets are not permanent elements of the urban hierarchy in the United States, although the system of fairs described by Kniffen does remain.

Elsewhere, fairs have changed their role. Some of the Central Andes fairs held in the Titicaca Basin towns have been completely abandoned. The pastoral type survived in its original form for the longest period, since the animals could be walked to market. Yet, in spite of their decline, fairs where the railways have penetrated are of dominant commercial importance.

Allix argued that as civilization perfects means of exchange and communication and assures the commercial world of increasing security,

[13] Belshaw, *Traditional Exchange and Modern Markets*.

conditions which support the commodity fair disappear and fairs must decline or suffer transformation. International traders cease to frequent fairs and abandon them completely to retail trade. Monetary transactions are carried on more and more by permanent exchanges and clearing houses. Merchandise is shipped only on order, while sales are made on sample (the sample fair). The system of fairs is superseded by wholesale trade. Large-scale commerce becomes rooted in permanent centers between which, in all directions and at all seasons, individuals, samples, and uninterrupted currents of goods flow.

The effect of this fixation of commerce, however, is not to diminish the number of fairs. Rather, as their importance declines, their number increases. Little local fairs arise which tend to degenerate into periodic amusements.

In the case of livestock fairs, Allix sees a similar decline. The rhythm of nomadism is no longer vital, so the fair whose *raison d'être* is pastoral nomadism is progressively losing its age-old importance. A more extensive clientele now demands a more regular supply, which the system of fairs does not provide. In addition, buyers of pastoral products increasingly tend to travel the mountains at all seasons and purchase directly from producers. The buyers seek to outdo each other and strive in particular to obtain the best of stock some days before the fairs. This decline of stock fairs has been slower than that of merchandise fairs, and Allix doubts that livestock fairs will disappear. The cattle fair, he believes, must survive as the best way of inspecting all the cattle of a region. In addition, stock-raisers can give only a limited portion of their time to buying and selling. Finally, the fairs still give the stock-raisers an opportunity for social intercourse and interregional exchange.

Change in Modern Urban Hierarchies

Once a modern hierarchy is established, it continues to change. According to Skinner's description of modern pre-Communist change in China, agrarian modernization took place prior to the spread of modern transportation. Once modern transportation was added, the lowest-level centers (standard markets) began to decline.

Commercialization enabled the peasants to market more often in higher-level centers, even before the coming of better roads, because of rising demands for imported goods. Better roads induced the villages to market their products in the higher-level centers providing these goods, bypassing the lowest-level centers. Links of higher-level centers to larger places, because of improved transport, reduced the price and increased the variety of goods available; increased trade permitted further differentiation and specialization; and decreasing activity put the lower-level centers in cumulatively less competitive situations. Schedules were reduced, and finally the lowest-level markets closed.

There was thus a reversal of traditional processes. Traditional change led to addition of centers, reductions in areas served, and growth at the lowest levels as functions moved down the hierarchy. Modern change decreased the number of centers, increased market area sizes, and forced functions upwards in the hierarchy. Expanding zones around growing cities in China were often undergoing modern changes and reductions in number of lower-level centers, while at the advancing edge modernization was taking place. Beyond the modern frontier, traditional processes worked to increase the number of centers and market schedules.

Modern change in the United States takes two forms, one the same kind as in China but more extreme, the other a function of spreading metropolitan regions. Throughout much of the country, as in the area of southwestern Iowa discussed in Chapter 1, initial entry of the railroad was instrumental in transforming a peasant economy into a commercial one, and within relatively few years thereafter the number of central places reached its maximum. Almost immediately complaints were heard of the death of hamlets and villages as a result of the spread of chain stores and the provision of farm-to-market roads. Chains avoided locating in the smallest centers, but better roads enabled farmers to journey to chains in the larger centers even before the automobile became widespread.[14]

The automobile, along with rising real incomes, accentuated these trends. Before 1930 hamlets with populations of 100 or less were declining; thereafter, as centralization of functions in higher levels of the hierarchy progressed, the general decline embraced villages with populations of less than 500. Today, the towns are moribund or declining, and all smaller central places continue to decline.

Two further forces accelerated these trends. In demand, mechanization of agriculture led to declining farm population, and in supply, scale shifts in retailing required many functions, like the chain stores before them, to be performed in larger centers than their predecessors.[15]

The net result has been both differential growth in importance of centers and selective thinning of central-place patterns. Between 1930 and 1960,[16] populations of central places in southwestern Iowa changed in the manner recorded in Table 6.1. There is a clear relation of population change to level of center in the hierarchy. By contrast, the rural farm population of the area fell at a rate of 0.28 per cent per annum, whereas the nation's metropolitan areas grew at a rate of 2.8 per cent.

These are average rates, combining a thinning out of the pattern by places dropping from one level to another in the hierarchy or ceasing to function altogether, and remaining places expanding their market areas to remain viable. Thus Hodge records transitions of centers from one level to another in Saskatchewan between 1941 and 1961 (Table 6.2).[17]

[14] Paul H. Landis, *South Dakota Town-Country Trade Relations, 1901–1931*, Bulletin 274, Agricultural Experiment Station, South Dakota State College, 1932.

[15] Douglas Chittick, *Growth and Decline of South Dakota Trade Centers, 1901–1951*, Bulletin 448, Agricultural Experiment Station, South Dakota State College, 1955.

[16] See Chapters 1 and 2.

[17] Gerald Hodge, *The Prediction of Trade Centre Viability in the Great Plains*, unpublished Ph.D. thesis, Mass. Institute of Technology, 1965.

Table 6.1.   Change of Central-Place Populations in Iowa,
1930–1960

Levels of center	Average annual growth rate (in per cent)
Hamlet	−2.69
Village	−0.58
Town	−0.15
County seat	+0.44
Regional city	+0.94

Note the preponderant drop in status of smaller central places. No less than 46 per cent of all hamlets died in the 20 year period.

Table 6.3 records other relevant data for Saskatchewan. Thinning of centers of town level and lower enabled remaining centers to increase the sizes of their trade areas, and thus their average spacing. Conversely, larger centers increased in number, and therefore their spacing decreased. In southwestern Iowa, the trade areas of lower-level centers increased in size from 1930 to 1960, accompanying the thinning out of the numbers of centers (Fig. 6.3). The trade area size increases were *exactly* those needed to keep the total populations served by the remaining low-level centers approximately constant over the interval (Fig. 6.4).

A second, increasingly important form of change in the United States is the spread of metropolitan regions. If centralization has characterized the performance of central functions and consumer travel, and if lower-level centers have declined or vanished, the rapid growth of regional cities and metropolitan areas has been accompanied by increasing sprawl of built-up areas and spread of metropolitan influences far into the countryside. In their excellent series of studies of the Upper Midwest, Borchert and his associates record some characteristics and implications

Table 6.2.   Changes in Proportion of Centers of Different
Levels, Saskatchewan, 1941–1961

		Class in 1961						
Class in 1941	Died by 1961	Hamlets	Villages	Towns	Smaller seats	County seats	Regional city	Regional capital
New centers	48	52						
Hamlets	46	52	2					
Villages	2	63	27	7	1			
Towns		6	28	39	26	1		
Smaller seats			2	19	63	16		
County seats					12	73	15	
Regional city							100	
Regional capital								100

Table 6.3. *Characteristics of Centers in Saskatchewan, 1961*

Classification	Number in 1961	Average spacing (in miles)	
		1941	1961
Hamlet	404	9.1	9.6
Village	150	10.3	13.5
Town	100	15.4	19.8
Small seat	85	25.9	22.5
County seat	29	40.4	39.5
Regional city	9	119.8	67.5
Regional capital	2	144.0	144.0

of the process.[18] They note the progressive shift of people from farm to non-farm occupations, from farms and small trade centers to large urban areas, and from built-up city areas into neighboring suburbs and countryside.

Metropolitan dispersal takes several forms. Most evident is the widening sprawl of suburbs outwards along improved highways and new expressways. Less obvious, but equally important, is the spread of the city's commuting area far beyond these suburbs, so that an increasing proportion of the scattered population is rural non-farm, or involves part-time farmers. The character of previously independent central places is transformed when the market served changes in this way.

Within the metropolitan region, specialization replaces the articulation of the central-place hierarchy. Some places continue in their central-place role, others become resorts or dormitory suburbs. New outlying shopping plazas are constructed, and business ribbons extend along highways. In short, the areas brought within expanding metropolitan regions are influenced by new locational forces and forms of interdependence, so the classical patterns of the central-place hierarchy break down and are replaced by business patterns characteristically internal to cities.[19] Expanding metropolitan regions are responsible for the same phase shift in the geography of retailing as attributed earlier to popula-

[18] John R. Borchert, *The Urbanization of the Upper Midwest: 1930–1960;* Borchert and Russell B. Adams, *Trade Centers and Trade Areas of the Upper Midwest;* Adams, *Population Mobility in the Upper Midwest;* Borchert, Thomas L. Anding, and Morris Gildemeister, *Urban Dispersal in the Upper Midwest* (University of Minnesota: Upper Midwest Economic Study, 1963–1964).

[19] See two of my articles in *Annals,* Association of American Geographers: "Ribbon Developments in the Urban Business Pattern," Vol. 49 (June 1959), 145–55; and "The Impact of Expanding Metropolitan Communities upon the Central Place Hierarchy," Vol. 50 (June 1950), 112–16. One of the first effects of expanding metropolitan influence is to reduce number of lowest-level centers at rates even more rapid than before. See Hodge, *op. cit.,* and Dwight Sanderson, *Rural Social and Economic Areas in Upstate New York,* Ithaca Agricultural Experiment Station Bulletin 614, 1934.

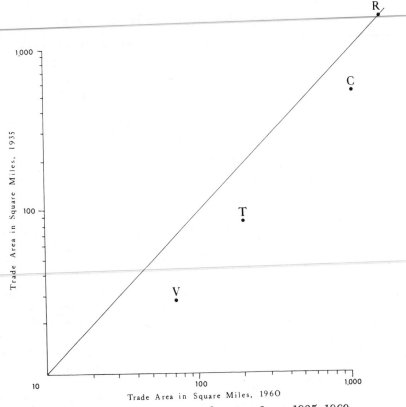

Fig. 6.3. *Trade area size changes in southwestern Iowa, 1935–1960.*

tion densities. The two are, of course, not unrelated. Since an increasing proportion of the North American population is becoming concentrated in such metropolitan regions, this current phase of modernization may be eliminating central-place hierarchies as we know them from the continent. The economic structure we can anticipate is a nation made up of a set of interdependent metropolitan regions, each region specialized to a high degree internally instead of being successively subdivided into progressively smaller regions to effectively articulate distribution of goods and services at retail.[20] Locational specialization, rather than the repetitive, nested levels of a central-place hierarchy, then becomes the key to understanding the most modern metropolitan forms of retail geography.

Change within Metropolitan Regions

The centers, ribbons, and specialized areas that comprise the retail geography of metropolitan regions are not unchanging, but undergo

20 Otis Dudley Duncan, *Metropolis and Region*; John R. P. Friedmann and John Miller, "The Urban Field," *Journal of the American Institute of Planners,* Vol. 31 (November 1965), 312–19.

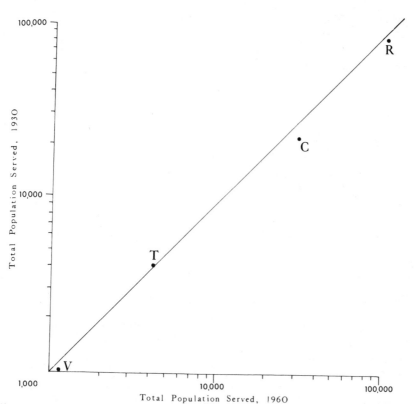

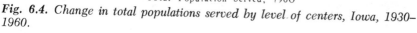

Fig. 6.4. Change in total populations served by level of centers, Iowa, 1930–1960.

continual adjustments in the short run and transformation in the longer run.

As metropolitan populations grow and redistribute themselves, retail facilities expand in areas where numbers of people are increasing, and contract where they are decreasing. Figure 6.5 shows how Chicago's population densities have systematically redistributed themselves over the years. Recently there has been a consistent decline in population in the inner city and growth at the periphery.[21] The result, seen in Figure 6.6, is a corresponding pattern of net decline of retail stores at the center and net growth at the periphery.

Population expansion and redistribution account for the over-all spatial *pattern* of retail change within the metropolitan region, but other factors

[21] For a thorough treatment of this pattern of density change, and the negative exponential distribution of densities with distance from the city center, see Berry, R. J. Tennant, and J. W. Simmons, "Urban Population Densities: Structure and Change," *Geographical Review*, Vol. 53 (July 1963), 389–405. Many studies have been completed related to the postwar central city-suburban redistribution of retail trade. A typical recent example is Homer Hoyt, "U. S. Metropolitan Area Retail Shopping Patterns," *Urban Land*, Vol. 25 (March 1966). One thorough general study is Eileen Schell, *Changes in Boston's Retail Landscape* (New York: Retail Research Institute, 1964).

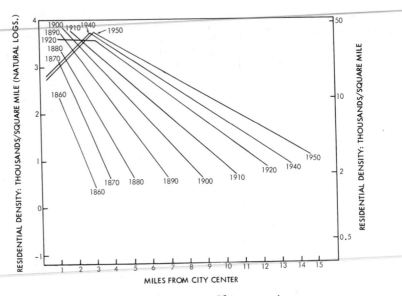

Fig. 6.5. *Change of population densities in Chicago region.*

affect the total *volume* of change. The importance of scale shifts in re-tailing and the attendant role of improvements in highway facilities have already been identified. Declines around the city center involve abandon-ments of older ribbon frontage, leaving vacant unwanted structures, whereas new growth at the periphery has led to construction of new planned shopping centers and larger ribbon stores.

Progressive increases in real incomes have also played their role, lead-ing to gradual increase in the proportion of stores devoted to specialties and shopping goods as opposed to convenience shops. The older un-planned centers and ribbons provide somewhat fewer facilities for higher income groups than the planned centers (Fig. 2.24), although there were always differences of this kind in the store composition of Chicago centers serving higher and lower income segments of the population.[22]

Results of the changes in retail technology are not as apparent in the central city, where most stores were constructed before the depression of the 1930's, as in the outlying sections of the metropolitan region. There, fingers of prewar development with their older unplanned centers and ribbons, together with more distant central places drawn within the metropolitan region as highway improvements have pushed the com-muting radius further out from the city center, have been faced with new suburban growth and modern planned shopping centers in the interstices between the developed fingers. Competition has been intense and the new planned centers, with larger, modern stores, more attractive ground plans, and ample free parking, have been the victors.

Change within the central cities has been of another kind. The cumula-

[22] Brian J. L. Berry, *Commercial Structure and Commercial Blight* (University of Chicago: Department of Geography Research Paper No. 85, 1963).

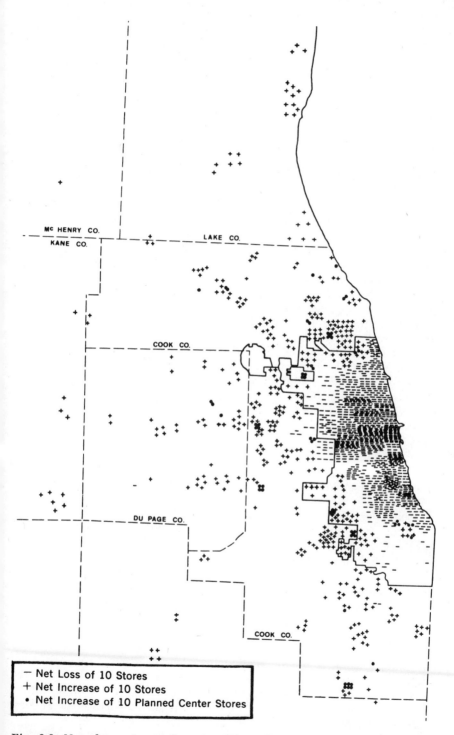

Fig. 6.6. Net change in number of retail establishments in Chicago region, 1948–1958.

121

tive effects of changing technology and declining population have been compounded by profound social change as the Negro has urbanized.

The classical picture of the social geography of an American city is one in which central areas provided homes for new immigrants who, as they prospered, moved outwards to wealthier neighborhoods. As the city grew, lower income neighborhoods extended outwards from the city center, encroaching upon the higher income zones. Urban ecologists have described these processes, using such concepts as "succession" and the "filtering down" of housing. There was one exception. It was other immigrants, not Negroes, who left the slums for better neighborhoods as their economic status improved. Negroes increased their residential area by gradual extension of the slums at their periphery. During the 1950's, however, the supply of housing caught up with the demand backlog created by the war. Negro population of northern cities multiplied by migration in patterns started during the war. In 1948 the United States Supreme Court ruled that "restrictive covenants" in property deeds could no longer be enforced to prevent the sale of houses to Negroes. The results in the Chicago example are clear. In 1940, out of a city population of 3.4 million, 300,000 were Negro and 3.1 million white. In 1950 the city's population reached 3.6 million, still with 3.1 million whites, but 500,-000 Negroes. In 1960 the white population had fallen to 2.7 million as the middle-income population fled to the suburbs, and the Negro population was over 800,000. Today, the number of Negro residents of Chicago approaches one million. What does this mean for retailing? Very simply, loss of markets, for Negro family income, because segregation has meant inferior education and restrictions in the job market, averages approximately two-thirds that of the white population of Chicago. Negro families are larger, and the incidence of unemployment (including a growing pool of technologically unemployed unskilled southern migrants and young high school dropouts) among Negroes is greater. Growth of the Negro population has meant declining retail markets throughout the city.

Combining longer-term shifts in technology, population redistribution, and social change, we find the following results in the neighborhoods of the City of Chicago:

1. If nothing else changed except consumer mobility and level of technology, the annual drop in number of retail establishments due to scale changes would be 5.87 per cent.

2. For every 1 per cent change in population there is a 0.98 per cent change in the number of retail units.

3. For every 1 per cent shift in real income levels, there is a 0.86 per cent change in the number of retail stores. Thus, social turnover from a middle-income white population to a low-income Negro population, which is accompanied by a 30 per cent drop in income levels in the decade from initial penetration of an area until it has completely "turned over," implies a decline of retail stores during the decade of at least 2.5 per cent per annum.

The exact process of retail transition during social change is interesting, because it holds the key to an understanding of the problem of commercial blight. There are several stages:

1. *The anticipation of neighborhood transition.* During this phase two important things happen. First, normal replacement of businesses which fail, or close because the owners retire or die, ceases. Vacancy rates begin to rise. Second, a "maintenance gap" appears. Property owners cease normal repairs, or reduce maintenance expenditures, because of growing uncertainty about prospective revenues. There are thus the beginnings of dilapidation, especially among vacant shops, and a generally run-down appearance prevails.

2. *During the period of population turnover.* In this phase demands drop precipitously, particularly for more specialized, higher quality goods. The more flexible stores change their price lines, but smaller, more specialized shops do not have such flexibility, and go out of business. Vacancies in centers rise, reaching between one-third and one-half the stores in the worst cases.

3. *The stabilization phase.* The neighborhood then settles down into its lower income character. There has been a maintenance gap, and now, with lower incomes, it is difficult to restore previously sound building conditions. The areas surrounding business centers are seedy and usually continue to deteriorate. Rents in the business centers drop, and the more viable establishments from the ribbons move in and fill up the vacant space. Vacancies mount in the ribbons, settling at around 20 per cent of all establishments, usually concentrated in the most dilapidated buildings, which, through lack of use, deteriorate even more. Lower income zones are thus criss-crossed with ribbons of unwanted, blighted commercial property.

The result is one of the most pressing planning problems in American cities today.

Emergence of New Metropolitan Forms

Locational specialization is the essence of the phase shift in retail geography within metropolitan areas. The classic hierarchy of central places is replaced by a pattern of business centers, ribbons, and specialized areas, with additional variations resulting from income differences or ethnicity. Further differentiation is added by contrasts in retail technology between unplanned developments of the pre-depression period and planned shopping centers, discount stores, and planned ribbons constructed since the end of World War II.

Some authors point to the emergence of new metropolitan forms accompanied by more extreme types of specialization.[23] They argue that the country is gradually becoming a set of metropolitan regions of 300,-000 or larger population located within two hours commuting time of a core area on modern expressway systems. The 300,000 figure was selected because Duncan said it marked a transition point at which "distinctly

[23] Friedmann and Miller, "The Urban Field."

metropolitan characteristics" appear.[24] Similarly, Thompson has said that areas of this size appear to have reached scales necessary for self-sustaining growth.[25]

These regions, it is argued, are far less focused than ever before, and the distinction between urban and rural no longer exists in them. Modern transportation and rising real incomes have removed the tyranny of distance, and people's life spaces (the areas in which they travel to work, shop, socialize, or use for recreation) have widened immensely. Shopping centers no longer dominate an immediate, exclusive market area; instead, several centers serve the same community-of-interest area, and consumers at some time visit all of them. Distance no longer provides protection. Centers must compete, and to achieve some margin of safety seek all means to differentiate themselves from their competitors (for example, by advertising and sales promotions). The only real safety is in the economies introduced by further specialization, and the result of widening of living spaces is to increase the locational specialization of individual functional areas and ribbons, and introduce specialization among shopping centers of the same level of the hierarchy.

The Christaller type of hierarchy thus breaks down. The new form of specialization said to be emerging has never been specified in the discussions. However, Lösch's model of non-hierarchical retail specialization may be applicable.

24 *Metropolis and Region.*
25 Wilbur Thompson, *A Preface to Urban Economics* (New York: Wiley, 1965).

PART 4 *mechanics of application*

CHAPTER SEVEN

Marketing geography

Marketing geography carries the retail interests of the geographer into practice within metropolitan areas, in the service of private business enterprises.

The need for such a geography was initially spelled out by its outstanding practitioner, William Applebaum,[1] who pointed out that the well-developed topical fields of economic geography were at that time, with the exception of transportation geography, concerned with production of material goods. But goods must not only be transported from production to consumption areas; they must also be transferred from the hands of producers, by collection and subsequent distribution, into the hands of consumers. This is the function of marketing. He argued that study of marketing had been neglected by geographers up to that time, in spite of the large section of working population engaged in marketing functions, the large part of urban landscape devoted to structures of wholesale and retail trade, and the complex channels of distribution leading from producing to consuming areas. A need in economic geography for marketing geography was evident, not only to strengthen other aspects of economic geography, but also to help the geographer in the marketing field contribute significantly to solutions of problems in the actual business of marketing. The scope of the field, Applebaum continued, should be delimitation and measurement of markets and study of the channels of distribution through which goods move from producers to consumers. The best place to develop marketing geography is in business, using the laboratory of actual business operations. The marketing problems to which the geographer can best apply the concepts

---

[1] William Applebaum, "Marketing Geography," *American Geography: Inventory and Prospect* (published for the Association of American Geographers by Syracuse Univ., 1954), pp. 245–51.

and procedures of his discipline are: (1) presenting market and marketing data; (2) evaluating markets; (3) delineating trading and selling areas; and (4) selecting channels of distribution and locations for wholesale, retail, or service establishments.

Less than ten years later, it was claimed in the introduction to a collection of papers that marketing geography had "come of age."[2] The papers had several characteristics in common. Concerned with actual business operations of firms, they discussed either the complete location research program of a firm or the retail growth program of a company with emphasis on selecting new store locations, or they focused on measuring the present or estimating the likely market areas, drawing power, and sales volumes of retail stores or shopping centers. Much of the emphasis was on how to conduct such studies. The final paper concluded with a plea for a better store location science. Store-site evaluation and store location research were recognized as more of an art than a science.[3] The solution, the authors said, could only be found in more facts, which might then be evaluated and integrated for more intelligent use, thereby supplying "material for broader concepts and theoretical formulations without which there is little science."[4]

Like many facets of geography, the work of the marketing geographers paid at best only lip service to the existence of a field of marketing and an expanding body of literature called marketing science, emanating from schools of business and economics. Schwartz points out that the genesis of serious study of marketing was approximately 1900, although this study initially produced a "plethora of facts that seem to add up to very little."[5] After World War II, however, a body of marketing theory emerged, so that one could in fact begin to talk of a marketing science.

That the marketing geographers should fail to build their work, after Applebaum's 1954 plea, within the framework of marketing science is understandable, since geography as a whole was for many years inward-looking and often insensitive to progress in related subjects.[6] What is surprising is that they should also have overlooked or rejected as "too abstract" the pioneering theoretical contribution of Christaller and the formalization of fundamental concepts by Lösch. If Schwartz provides a picture of the diversity and lack of integration of the theoretical bases of marketing science, Christaller and Lösch presented a consistent frame for delineating trading areas, selecting retail locations, presenting marketing data, and evaluating markets. Twenty years before Applebaum prepared his paper on marketing geography, a theoretical frame had been developed *within geography!*

[2] Raymond E. Murphy, "Marketing Geography Comes of Age," introduction to *Store Location and Development Studies,* a volume of reprints from *Economic Geography* (Worcester: Clark Univ., 1961).
[3] Saul B. Cohen and William Applebaum, "Evaluating Store Sites and Determining Store Rents," *ibid.,* p. 95.
[4] *Ibid.*
[5] George Schwartz, *Development of Marketing Theory.*
[6] See the development of this thought in National Academy of Sciences–National Research Council, *The Science of Geography,* Publication 1277, 1965.

Marketing Geography

The prime concern of marketing geographers, tying together their several interests, is in *how to measure a trading area.*[7] Such measurement is the basis of presenting marketing data, evaluating store or shopping center performance, studying changes due to new competition (implicit in all the discussions of shopping centers is a three-level hierarchy: neighborhood, community, and regional), or estimating the locational advantages and potential earnings of new sites for stores or centers.

A consistent procedure is used by all marketing geographers for market area measurement. The first step is to prepare a population dot map of an area, and place over the map a grid of squares of ¼-mile, ⅛-mile, or ¹⁄₁₆-mile on the sides, depending upon fineness of detail desired. Customers are then interviewed in the stores of interest, and located by place of residence within the appropriate grid-cell. Sample size is established for the interviewing by average weekly store sales: one customer for every $100 sales. By dividing the number of customers in each grid cell by the population of that cell, and multiplying by $100, the *per capita weekly sales* to residents of the area in the store is obtained.

The *drawing power* of the store is calculated by finding the proportion of sample customers within successive distance bands (¼-mile, ½-mile) or within successive increments of travel time (5 minutes, 10 minutes). By multiplying the number of samples by $100, weekly sales within each band are computed.

In the same way, *market penetration* is derived. Census tract statistics in the *U.S. Census of Population and Housing* relate the median income of families in each grid cell. The Bureau of Labor Statistics' reports on *Consumer Expenditures and Income* provide per capita weekly home expenditures for the income group, for the commodities sold by the store. By dividing the actual per capita expenditures of consumers in the store by the BLS figure, the proportional *market share* of the store in expenditures of consumers in the grid cell is obtained.

Two isoline maps can result. One shows the accumulative percentage of total store sales with increasing distance or time from the store; the other shows declining market shares with increasing distance or time. Comparison of these maps enables the *primary, secondary,* and *fringe trading areas* of stores to be identified. For supermarkets, the primary trading area generally comprises areas from which 60 to 70 per cent of the trade comes and where the market penetration of the store is greater than that of competitors; the secondary area is that from which the next 20 to 30 per cent is derived, and the fringe covers the balance. Consistent application of these isoline values provides an excellent pic-

---

[7] William Applebaum, "How to Measure the Value of a Trading Area," *Chain Store Age* (November 1940), 92–94, 111–14; Applebaum and Richard F. Spears, "How to Measure a Trading Area," *Chain Store Age* (January 1951), 149–54. A systematic treatment of the process is provided by Bernard J. Kane, Jr., *A Systematic Guide to Supermarket Location Analysis* (New York: Fairchild Publications, 1966).

ture of supermarket territories in a community, although the exact isoline values should vary by size of store, according to the center in which the store is located, and by type of business.[8]

Changes in trading area maps and related statistics between time periods make it possible to assess and quantify the effects of population and highway changes, new competition, or store and business center improvements on drawing power and market penetration. Where potential new store sites have to be evaluated, drawing power and market penetration maps make possible the estimation of potential primary trading areas reachable from the new sites, and calculation of needed store size and likely sales volumes and profits.[9] Such is the basis of practice in marketing geography.[10]

Relevant Aspects of Marketing Science

Analogous practices and a host of related rule-of-thumb procedures have been developed by store location practitioners. The most noteworthy summary of this work is by Nelson,[11] who discusses in his survey the effects of location on retailing, selection of a location, techniques of estimating business volumes, analysis of a three-level hierarchy of shopping centers (neighborhood, community, and regional), and new trends in the economics of location.

Paralleling the work of consulting practitioners has been the gradual emergence of a science of marketing in university schools of business and economics.

The first important contribution related to marketing geography was the attempt by Reilly to develop the general "laws" of retail gravitation [12] that were reviewed in Chapter 2. There have been many attempts to improve upon Reilly's laws, for example by Converse,[13] with but little success until the recent work of Huff.

Huff's model, as presented in Chapter 2, states that the probability that a customer located at A will visit store 1 is

$$p_{A1} = \frac{\dfrac{S_1}{T_{A1}^{\alpha}}}{\sum\limits_{i=1}^{r} \left(\dfrac{S_i}{T_{A1}^{\alpha}} \right)}$$

[8] William Applebaum and Saul B. Cohen, "Store-Location Strategy in a Changing Market," *Proceedings of the 1961 Mid-Year Conference*, Super Market Institute, 1961.

[9] For the existing stores in a chain, relevant equations can be fitted to the data and then used to make predictions for new store locations.

[10] Examples of this practice include *Store Location and Development Studies* and the studies by Applebaum, Cohen, and Spears already cited. Also Applebaum, *Patterns of Food Distribution in the Metropolis* (Chicago: Super Market Institute, 1966); and Schell, *Changes in Boston's Retail Landscape*.

[11] Richard Lawrence Nelson, *The Selection of Retail Locations* (Chicago: Dodge, 1958). See also Kane's *Systematic Guide to Supermarket Location Analysis*.

[12] William J. Reilly, *Methods for the Study of Retail Relationships*, Research Monograph No. 4 of the Bureau of Business Research, University of Texas, 1929.

[13] Paul D. Converse, "New Laws of Retail Gravitation," *Journal of Marketing*, Vol. 14 (October 1949).

where S indicates store size and T travel time. Consistent application of the model provides a picture of the market penetration of each store (Fig. 2.16). Further, for any store j and area i, where C_i is the total number of consumers residing in i, and W_k is average weekly expenditures on the product of interest for income group k, $P_{ij}C_i$ gives total customers coming to store j from area i, and $P_{ij}C_iW_k$ measures the sales accruing to the store from that area. Summation over all areas provides a measure of total trade.

Huff argues that his model provides very good replications of actual behavior, and he has programmed it for routine solution on a large computer.[14] Since his formulation stems, not from Reilly's empirical rules, but from a reasonable theory of individual choice behavior,[15] it has sound foundations. Most important, this recent contribution from marketing science provides, in a single consistent frame, a basis for the practice of marketing geographers, which it replicates. Marketing science now has many other bodies of theory,[16] but Huff's formulation is of the greatest use to marketing geographers.

Central-Place Theory as a Base

The marketing geographer's map showing declines of per capita sales with distance from a store depicts a spatial demand cone. The map of primary trading areas derived from a composite presentation of market penetration of a set of retail units shows the equivalent in a variable city environment of hexagons on a uniform plain. Drawing power calculations that result in an estimate of total sales for a potential new store location are the equivalent of integrating beneath a demand cone. *The practice of marketing geography is to produce the basic figures required in central-place theory.* To reverse the argument, a theoretical framework for prac-

[14] David L. Huff and Larry Blue, *A Programmed Solution for Estimating Retail Sales Potentials* (Lawrence, Kansas: Center for Regional Studies, 1966).

[15] *Determination of Intra-Urban Retail Trade Areas.* Briefly, where (1) there is a set J of alternative shopping centers or stores, and (2) the utility derived by a consumer from alternative j is u_j, the model states that: (3) the probability p_j of alternative j being chosen from J is proportional to u_j, or

$$p_j = \frac{u_j}{\sum\limits_j u_j}$$

and $\sum\limits_j p_j = 1.0$ with $0 < p_j < 1$.

(4) Probabilities of choice are independent of existence of other centers; therefore

$$\frac{p_i}{p_k} = \frac{u_i}{u_k}$$

(5) The utility of a center or store is directly proportional to the ratio S_j/T_{ij}^α where T_j is the travel time from the consumer's residence i to j, so that

$$p_{ij} = \frac{\dfrac{S_i}{T_{ij}^\alpha}}{\sum\limits_j \left(\dfrac{S_i}{T_{ij}^\alpha} \right)}$$

[16] Schwartz, *Development of Marketing Theory.*

tice therefore exists. Huff's model of consumer behavior, in integrating the practice, provides probabilistic rules from which central-place theory may be generalized within the urban scene, to allow for complex over-lapping market areas. If existing theory provides a way to make sense of practice, there are also all the ingredients for the long experience of the practitioner to be formalized and brought to bear to improve the theory, through the medium of new, integrative models.

CHAPTER EIGHT

Planning uses

Planners consistently make use of the concept of an urban hierarchy and related facets of regional organization. When the Dutch planned settlements to serve farms newly established on polders reclaimed from the Ijsselmeer, they created a two-level hierarchy of market centers for the farmers. On the Lakhish plains running eastward from the Gaza strip, Israel built a system of new settlements in a three-level hierarchy:

A settlements of various kinds (including protective border *kibbutzim*) absorbing immigrant settlers and Israeli pioneers, and serving as centers of agricultural cultivation, containing facilities used daily by the settlers.

B settlements (rural community centers), each planned to serve 4 to 6 A settlements and to supply facilities and buildings used by them once or twice a week.

C (regional center), a town roughly at the geographical center of the region, providing administrative, educational, medical and cultural facilities, and with factories for processing crops.[1]

Analysis of the pattern of shopping centers and identification of their service areas provided one of the main ingredients in the administrative reorganization of Greater London.[2] When the village of Park Forest, Illinois, was laid out as a planned suburban community, residential areas were organized into neighborhoods, each served by a local business center, and the whole community was provided with one larger shopping

---

[1] *Operation Lakhish. Stage 2,* a publication of the United Israel Appeal (n.d.). Lösch notes that Christaller's formulation similarly influenced German regional planning. See *The Economics of Location,* pp. 131–33, fn. 16.

[2] *Report of the Royal Commission on Local Government in Greater London, 1957–60* (London: HMSO, Cmnd. 1164). Also W. I. Carruthers, "Service Centres in Greater London," *The Town Planning Review,* Vol. 33 (April 1962), 7–31.

center, with adjacent land reserved for the administrative services of village hall, police, and fire departments.[3]

These examples are symbolic of the practical uses of the central-place *idea* by regional and city planners for locating retail business, business centers, and market towns, or regionalizing an area. More recently, work has been undertaken explicitly within the framework of the *theory:* for example, in deliberations of the Royal Commission on Agriculture and Rural Life in Saskatchewan; in considering the needed changes in the urban structure of Ghana; in developing models to aid the attack on commercial blight in the Chicago or Toronto regions; or in constructing a general theory of regional planning.[4]

Regional Planning: Examples

The basic argument supporting use of central-place ideas in regional planning is that a system of centers arranged in a hierarchy provides an efficient way of articulating distribution to, and administration of, regions. A proper system can avoid duplication and waste, and make possible the realization of social benefits accruing from economies of scale. Identification of a network of centers and the scale of activities appropriate to each level makes possible the proper location of new facilities, or, where the scale of enterprise is changing rapidly, a systematic base for rationalization. Where an existing system is an integral part of the social and economic life of an area, it must be considered in any replanning efforts, or the efforts are doomed to failure. Conversely, it can be argued that the very leadership of major central places, as *growth poles,* sets the pace of progress of their regions.[5]

Consider first cases in North America. In Saskatchewan the distribution of population is changing rapidly as agriculture continues to mechanize, mobility of farmers increases, and scale of business changes. The Royal Commission report argued that central-place concepts provide an understanding of the networks and hierarchies within which these changes are taking place, expressing the interdependencies among places that are of continuing significance for the provision of such public services as health,

---

[3] The distinction between neighborhood, community, and regional centers has been fundamental to planned shopping plaza development since the end of World War II. See G. Baker and B. Funaro, *Shopping Centers* (New York: Reinhold, 1951), or W. Burns, *British Shopping Centres* (London: Hill, 1959).

[4] Royal Commission on Agriculture and Rural Life, Saskatchewan, *Service Centers* (Regina: Queen's Printer, 1957); D. Grove and L. Huszar, *The Towns of Ghana* (Accra: Ghana Univ., 1964); Berry, *Commercial Structure and Commercial Blight* and *Metropolitan Planning Guidelines: Commercial Structure;* J. W. Simmons, *Toronto's Changing Retail Complex: A Study in Growth and Blight,* Department of Geography Research Paper No. 104, University of Chicago, 1966; E. von Böventer, "Spatial Organization Theory as a Basis for Regional Planning," *Journal of the American Institute of Planners,* Vol. 30 (1964), 90–100.

[5] François Perroux, *L'Économie du xxᵉ siècle* (Paris: Presses Universitaires, 1961); J. R. Boudeville, "Hiérarchie urbaine et aménagement des villes," *Revue d'Économie Politique,* Vol. 74 (January 1964), 65–92.

education, and municipal government. As the optimal scale of services shifts, the levels of centers provide an organized way of choosing new service locations, and also specify places where inefficient services are to be terminated. For new programs, the optimum size involves analysis of program objectives, planning requirements, administrative loads, public participation, and technical efficiency, but the central-place system then provides proper locations. Where administration requires several levels, the levels of the central-place hierarchy are available.

Changes of like order are taking place in Iowa, calling for extensive relocation of facilities.[6] A typical example is the state's agricultural extension services. Today, each of the more than 90 counties has its extension agent, but the system is becoming increasingly inefficient. It is proposed to rationalize the system by concentrating agents into a dozen regional centers, each serving multi-county "functional economic areas." Each of these areas is not only a relatively self-contained area with respect to shopping trips of inhabitants, but is a "labor market" too, with relatively few commuters crossing its borders, making an ideal unit for social accounting purposes at the regional level.[7] Each is also the service area of a center at the "regional city" level of the hierarchy.

An extension of the argument in many countries is that where there is disjunction between the boundaries of administrative areas and those of service areas of central places, the latter should be used for local government replanning.[8]

In developing countries there are other problems. Towns are growing in size and absorbing greater proportions of the total population, while technical improvements are changing rural life; the relations of town and country are being reordered. New and growing towns make more demands on the country, while changing rural areas demand more technical services, educational, health, and entertainment facilities, and greater supplies of goods and services from the towns. Regional planning seeks to administer these relationships and foster the change through the central role of urban centers as focal points in the diffusion of expectations and innovations.[9] Identification of a hierarchy in such countries makes possible the evaluation of the system within which change is to take place. Regions with insufficiently developed networks may find establishment of new centers a priority activity. Availability of a proper hierarchy enables rational planning of facilities to proceed, without waste, at the correct scales. Establishment of a new center or upgrading an old

[6] Karl A. Fox, "The Major Problem of Rural Society," *Our Rural Problems in Their National Setting* (Ames: Iowa State Univ., 1962), pp. 9–26; and "Delineating Functional Economic Areas," *Research and Education for Regional and Area Development* (Ames: Iowa State Univ., 1966), pp. 13–55.

[7] Fox, *ibid.*

[8] F. H. W. Green, "Community of Interest and Local Government Areas," *Public Administration*, Vol. 34 (January 1956), 39–49.

[9] Grove and Huszar, *The Towns of Ghana.* Similar views are expressed in Reed Moyer, *Marketing in Economic Development,* International Business Occasional Paper No. 1, Michigan State University, 1965.

one can provide a powerful stimulus to development of the surrounding area, setting the pace for its progress.

India is a country in which economic isolation of villages is particularly apparent. The present link with urban centers is one-sided. While rural poverty is deepening, villagers drift aimlessly to nearby towns in search of employment. The towns, in consequence, grow but do not develop, and rural squalor is extended into urban slums. A solution proposed by India's National Council for Applied Economic Research is development of a sufficient number of market towns to provide improved facilities for buying and selling by the villagers, and to serve them in other economic and social ways.[10] Specifically, it has been proposed to develop India's "regulated markets" by filling out the pattern spatially, and making selective investments to create an appropriate infrastructure and the attunement of road, electricity, warehouse, and industrial estate development in concert.

This is in contrast with Communist planning in China,[11] the main elements of which were land reform, and socialization of rural trade via state trading companies and supply and marketing cooperatives. Initially, these institutions worked within the periodic marketing system, controlling the supply of goods and approximately half the sales in rural markets. But in August 1958, the regime made a major shift to the left, and merged the supply and marketing cooperatives while abolishing the traditional institutions of peasant marketing.[12] The result was near paralysis in commodity distribution. After attempts to realign marketing systems with administrative units,[13] the natural economic systems were gradually restored. Although from 1958 to 1963 the cooperatives had discouraged circulation of itinerants, "assistants" of the cooperatives began to reinstitute traditional circuits thereafter. With current transport improvements the standard markets are gradually being eliminated, and trade is being concentrated in the upper two levels. Paralleling rehabilitation of periodic marketing, communes that had been the leaders of land reform were subdivided into units approximating standard marketing systems. As a result, the traditional Chinese village is being brought intact into the modern world as a "production brigade," while the standard marketing community also exhibits continuities. The standard market towns remain as "basic-level supply points," meeting according to traditional schedules; and the funneling and supply functions of intermediate towns

[10] E. A. J. Johnson, *Market Towns and Spatial Development in India* (New Delhi: National Council of Applied Economic Research, 1965).

[11] The following is the interpretation of Skinner in "Marketing and Social Structure in Rural China."

[12] In the Soviet Union there is complete central control of the distribution system, through retail enterprises of the Union Republic Trade Ministries, Company Stores, Supply Bases, and Consumer Cooperatives. For discussions of the Soviet case see Marshall I. Goldman, "Product Differentiation and Advertising: Some Lessons from Soviet Experience," *Journal of Political Economy*, Vol. 68 (June 1960), 346–57; and "The Cost and Efficiency of Distribution in the Soviet Union," *Quarterly Journal of Economics*, Vol. 76 (July 1962), 437–53.

[13] China traditionally had two hierarchies, one for administration and one for marketing.

and bulking and wholesale functions of central market towns are preserved, even though state agencies now perform them. The existing system thus constrained China's Communist planning, which is now working with a traditional system of regional organization.

City Planning for Business Centers

F. Stuart Chapin's textbook on city planning [14] accepts as given a familiar three-level hierarchy of neighborhood-serving, community-serving, and region-serving shopping centers, plus a special class of highway-serving uses. He relates the classification to the relevant theory, and sees as the main tasks of land use planning the establishment of location and space requirements for such centers, and their subsequent incorporation into some over-all plan.

Location requirements include, according to Chapin:

Regional business centers: Location on main arterial highways, site adequate for peak parking needs and sufficient services to fill several hours of a shopper's time.

Community-serving centers: On major thoroughfare, located on in-town edge of trade area.

Neighborhood centers: Within convenient walking distance of families served.[15]

Space requirements can be computed by determining dollar demands accruing to centers, and the sales area needed to meet the demands, together with total site areas needed to support the given sales areas. Detailed procedures for estimation are set forth, somewhat akin to the marketing geographers' procedure for measuring trading areas. Figure 8.1 presents a nomograph setting on parallel scales the outcome of one such exercise.[16] A horizontal line drawn across the figure at any market area size will produce needed space requirements and other center features. Figures 8.2 and 8.3 show some of the relationships from which such nomographs can be derived, for unplanned and planned centers. See also Figures 2.11 and 2.12.

This conventional outline is presented sketchily because it is such a familiar part of the activity of every department of city planning and the training of every planning student that many descriptive texts are available detailing the procedures.[17] Related to, and proceeding from, the

[14] *Urban Land Use Planning* (Urbana: Univ. of Illinois, 1965).
[15] Hans Carol, "Der Standort des 'Shopping Center,'" *Plan*, Vol. 22 (November–December 1965), 208–14, relates location to the central-place scheme.
[16] From Berry, *Commercial Structure and Commercial Blight.*
[17] See Nelson, *The Selection of Retail Locations*, for example. A more sophisticated modern approach is provided by T. R. Lakshmanan and W. G. Hansen, "A Retail Market Potential Model," *Journal of the American Institute of Planners*, Vol. 31 (September 1965), 134–43.

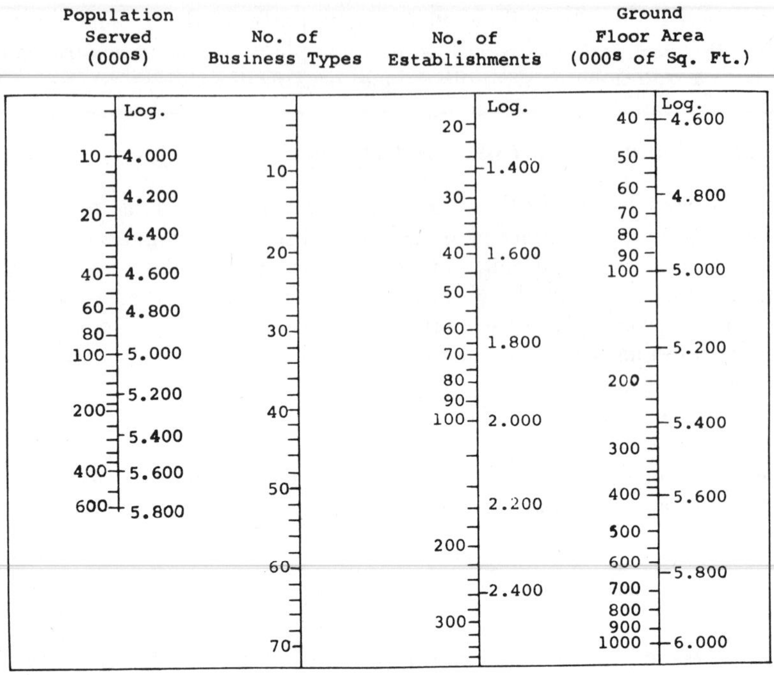

Population Served (000ˢ)	No. of Business Types	No. of Establishmentṣ	Ground Floor Area (000ˢ of Sq. Ft.)

Fig. 8.1. Relations between market-area characteristics: centers in lower-income areas of Chicago.

conventional concept and resulting plan are city zoning ordinances that reserve certain tracts of land for business centers of each kind. Effective administration of the zoning ordinance is the means whereby the land use planner attempts to achieve his plan.

But he can only hope for complete effectuation if he can plan in developing areas, forcing the pattern of retail locations into his preestablished mould. Where a system exists and is transforming internally, he must adjust to it. Where a system is declining, his best activity is to attempt to remove excess capacity causing commercial blight,[18] or to change the nature of the changing market that is causing blight.

Conclusion

Planning uses of the central-place framework are piecemeal, for the central-place concept has yet to be systematically incorporated into planning models. If the reality of empirical regularities is accepted, convergence of the regularities and deductions from theory acknowledged, and parallelism of cross-cultural differences and historical sequences ad-

[18] Berry, *Commercial Structure and Commercial Blight,* and "The Retail Component of the Urban Model," *Journal of the American Institute of Planners,* Vol. 31 (September 1965), 150–55.

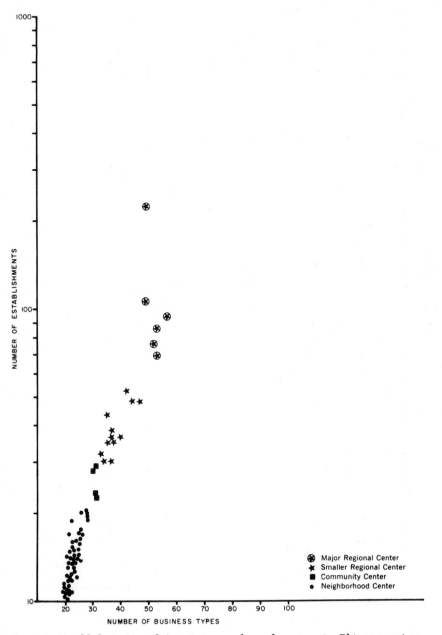

Fig. 8.2. Establishments and functions: unplanned centers in Chicago region.

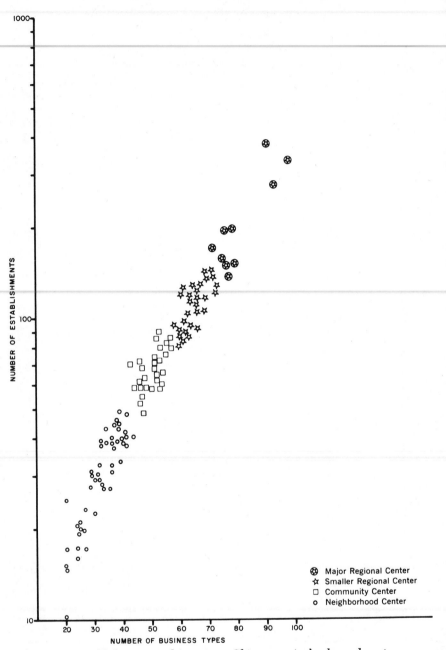

Fig. 8.3. Establishments and functions: Chicago region's planned centers.

mitted, any programmatic activity directed at retail location must take note of it, however. Whether the effort be to find new drugstore locations in growing North American suburbs, rationalize public services in Saskatchewan, plan new market centers on the polders, or identify growth poles in the regional planning of India, the ideas presented concerning the economic geography of the distribution system must play an increasingly significant role.

Index

Brian J. L. Berry is Professor of Geography and Director of Training
Programs of the Center for Urban Studies at The University of Chicago.
Born in England, he received his undergraduate education at University
College, London, and his Ph.D. at The University of Washington, Seattle.
He is the author of several books, among them *Studies of Highway
Development and Geographic Change, Commercial Structure and
Commercial Blight*, and *Essays on Commodity Flows and the Spatial
Structure of the Indian Economy*. In addition, he has written many articles
published in journals of geography, urban studies, and planning.

Prentice-Hall Foundations of Economic Geography Series

NORTON GINSBURG, *editor*

geography of manufacturing,   GUNNAR ALEXANDERSSON

geography of market centers and retail distribution,   BRIAN J. L. BERRY

geography of natural resources,   IAN BURTON and ROBERT W. KATES

geography of agriculture,   HOWARD GREGOR

geography of energy,   NATHANIEL B. GUYOL

geography of urban land use,   HAROLD MAYER

geography of water resources,   W. R. DERRICK SEWELL

geography of transportation,   EDWARD J. TAAFFE and HOWARD L. GAUTHIER, JR.

geography of international trade,   RICHARD S. THOMAN and EDGAR C. CONKLING

geography of wholesaling,   JAMES E. VANCE, JR.

a prologue to population geography,   WILBUR ZELINSKY

3513